MANUFACTURING TECHNOLOGY RESEARCH

U.S. MANUFACTURING DOGFIGHTS

CHINA'S STEEL AND FOREIGN AIRCRAFT COMPETITION

Manufacturing Technology Research

Additional books in this series can be found on Nova's website under the Series tab.

Additional E-books in this series can be found on Nova's website under the E-books tab.

Business Issues, Competition and Entrepreneurship

Additional books in this series can be found on Nova's website under the Series tab.

Additional E-books in this series can be found on Nova's website under the E-books tab.

MANUFACTURING TECHNOLOGY RESEARCH

U.S. MANUFACTURING DOGFIGHTS

CHINA'S STEEL AND FOREIGN AIRCRAFT COMPETITION

JEFFREY A. BALL
EDITOR

Nova Science Publishers, Inc.
New York

Copyright © 2012 by Nova Science Publishers, Inc.

All rights reserved. No part of this book may be reproduced, stored in a retrieval system or transmitted in any form or by any means: electronic, electrostatic, magnetic, tape, mechanical photocopying, recording or otherwise without the written permission of the Publisher.

For permission to use material from this book please contact us:
Telephone 631-231-7269; Fax 631-231-8175
Web Site: http://www.novapublishers.com

NOTICE TO THE READER

The Publisher has taken reasonable care in the preparation of this book, but makes no expressed or implied warranty of any kind and assumes no responsibility for any errors or omissions. No liability is assumed for incidental or consequential damages in connection with or arising out of information contained in this book. The Publisher shall not be liable for any special, consequential, or exemplary damages resulting, in whole or in part, from the readers' use of, or reliance upon, this material. Any parts of this book based on government reports are so indicated and copyright is claimed for those parts to the extent applicable to compilations of such works.

Independent verification should be sought for any data, advice or recommendations contained in this book. In addition, no responsibility is assumed by the publisher for any injury and/or damage to persons or property arising from any methods, products, instructions, ideas or otherwise contained in this publication.

This publication is designed to provide accurate and authoritative information with regard to the subject matter covered herein. It is sold with the clear understanding that the Publisher is not engaged in rendering legal or any other professional services. If legal or any other expert assistance is required, the services of a competent person should be sought. FROM A DECLARATION OF PARTICIPANTS JOINTLY ADOPTED BY A COMMITTEE OF THE AMERICAN BAR ASSOCIATION AND A COMMITTEE OF PUBLISHERS.

Additional color graphics may be available in the e-book version of this book.

Library of Congress Cataloging-in-Publication Data
U.S. manufacturing dogfights : China's steel and foreign aircraft competition / editor, Jeffrey A. Ball.
    p. cm.
  Includes index.
  ISBN 978-1-62100-672-5 (softcover)
  1. Aerospace industries--United States. 2. Aerospace industries--China. 3. Airbus Industrie. 4. Boeing Aerospace Company. 5. Competition, International. I. Ball, Jeffrey A. II. Title: US manufacturing dogfights.
  HD9711.5.U62U24 2011
  338.4'76291333--dc23
                                                                                        2011037646

Published by Nova Science Publishers, Inc. † New York

CONTENTS

Preface		vii
Chapter	China's Steel Industry and Its Impact on the United States: Issues for Congress *Rachel Tang*	1
Chapter 2	Challenge to the Boeing-Airbus Duopoly in Civil Aircraft: Issues for Competitiveness *Glennon J. Harrison*	37
Index		77

PREFACE

This book provides an overview of China's steel industry and discusses the issues and implications with regard to the U.S. steel sector.

Chapter 1- China's steel industry has grown significantly since the mid-1990s. China is now the world's largest steelmaker and steel consumer. In 2009, China produced over 567 million tons of crude steel, nearly half of the world's steel. That was 10 times the U.S. production.

The majority of Chinese steel has been used to meet domestic demand in China. However, as its steel production continues to grow, overcapacity is becoming a major concern to Chinese industrial policy makers, as well as steelmakers outside China. Although industry statistics indicate that the Chinese steel industry is not export-oriented, its consistently high output keeps U.S. steelmakers concerned that excess Chinese steel might overwhelm the global market once domestic demand is adequately met. These concerns become increasingly acute as the United States and the rest of the world are in the middle of a slow recovery from the economic recession started in December 2007.

Chapter 2- The importance of a successful aerospace industry to the United States economy has been repeatedly acknowledged by President Obama and members of his Cabinet, many Members of Congress, and by all concerned with the competitive fortunes of the U.S. aircraft manufacturing industry. The U.S. aerospace industry is highly competitive and global in scope. U.S. firms manufacture a wide range of products for civil and defense purposes and, in 2010, the value of aerospace industry shipments was estimated at $171 billion, of which civil aircraft and aircraft parts accounted for over half of all U.S. aerospace shipments. In 2010, the U.S. aerospace industry exported nearly $78 billion in products, of which $67 billion (or 86%

of total exports) were civil aircraft, engines, equipment, and parts. The U.S. trade surplus (net exports) in aerospace products in 2010 was $43.6 billion – higher than for any other manufacturing industry. Aerospace employment totaled 477,000 workers, of which 228,400 were engaged in the manufacture of aircraft, 76,400 in the manufacture of engines and engine parts, and 97,600 in the manufacture of other parts and equipment. According to the International Trade Administration, "more jobs in the United States were supported by exports of U.S. aerospace products than of any other manufacturing or service industry."

In: U.S. Manufacturing Dogfights
Editors: Jeffrey A. Ball

ISBN: 978-1-62100-672-5
© 2012 Nova Science Publishers, Inc

Chapter 1

CHINA'S STEEL INDUSTRY AND ITS IMPACT ON THE UNITED STATES: ISSUES FOR CONGRESS[*]

Rachel Tang

SUMMARY

China's steel industry has grown significantly since the mid-1990s. China is now the world's largest steelmaker and steel consumer. In 2009, China produced over 567 million tons of crude steel, nearly half of the world's steel. That was 10 times the U.S. production.

The majority of Chinese steel has been used to meet domestic demand in China. However, as its steel production continues to grow, overcapacity is becoming a major concern to Chinese industrial policy makers, as well as steelmakers outside China. Although industry statistics indicate that the Chinese steel industry is not export-oriented, its consistently high output keeps U.S. steelmakers concerned that excess Chinese steel might overwhelm the global market once domestic demand is adequately met. These concerns become increasingly acute as the United States and the rest of the world are in the middle of a slow recovery from the economic recession started in December 2007.

---

[*] This is an edited, reformatted and augmented version of a Congressional Research Service publication, CRS Report for Congress R41421, from www.crs.gov, dated September 21, 2010.

The Chinese steel industry is highly fragmented, with more than 1,000 steel producers, which makes the domestic market highly competitive and difficult to control. Its growth also faces constraints such as dependence on imported iron ore and high energy consumption. The Chinese government has shown interest in stepping up its efforts to rein in steel overcapacity and to consolidate and restructure the steel industry. However, it remains to be seen if the government's efforts and measures are to produce sufficient or meaningful results.

The possibility of surplus steel from Chinese steel producers; their alleged questionable, if not illegal, trade practices; and the possibility of Chinese direct investment in the U.S. steel sector are all of major concern to the steelmakers in the United States.

Steelmakers in the United States believe that China's government subsidization of its steel (in the form of an undervalued currency, export rebates and/or quotas, subsidized financing, relatively weak environmental, labor, and safety regulations, etc.) is one of the key issues affecting the health of the U.S. steel sector. There have been multiple anti-dumping and countervailing cases in the United States against certain Chinese steel products, which suggests that U.S. steel producers and trade officials are increasingly using trade remedies to enforce international trade laws.

The rise of China's steel sector, along with other manufacturing industries, presents issues beyond trade law enforcement. China's quest for industrial raw materials is having considerable effect on global demand and supply, and as a result, the prices and availability of such inputs. China's restrictions on exports of some raw materials, allegedly, lower the cost of such raw materials in the home economy, while increasing global prices of these products (or diminishing global supply), thereby producing an unfair advantage in some manufacturing industries.

Amid the rising trade cases against various Chinese steel imports, Congress became increasingly concerned over alleged unfair trade competition from China. In August 2010, legislative measures were introduced in the Senate (S. 3725), while a set of measures focusing on illegal import practices were proposed by the U.S. Commerce Department, both aiming to continue the rigorous and more effective enforcement of U.S. trade laws.

This report provides an overview of China's steel industry and discusses the issues and implications with regard to the U.S. steel sector.

INTRODUCTION

China has become an increasingly prominent economic and political power, especially during the first decade of the 21st century. Since 1978, the year that officially marked the beginning of China's economic reform, China and its steel industry have experienced rapid economic development. In the 31-year time period between 1978 and 2009, the real GDP growth rate of China averaged 9%.[1] China's emergence as a major economic power is a key factor in understanding and forecasting the global steel markets and prices.

The global economic downturn, which began in December 2007, has considerably dampened industrial growth in developed countries. However, China continues its rapid economic development, in part propelled by the government's fiscal stimulus package aimed at building infrastructure and spurring domestic demand. China's economic growth in the second half of 2009 and in early 2010, reportedly, was fueled by a massive increase in bank lending.[2]

Questions remain concerning how long China can manage to sustain such rapid economic growth rates. Concerned about an overheated economy, which could result in high inflation, the Chinese central government recognized the need for a measured slowdown of its economic growth. In mid-April 2010, the Chinese government introduced a package of measures to discourage property speculation and, therefore, to prevent a possible property market bubble. Meanwhile, the central government also ordered the banking sector to limit lending to local government infrastructure projects.[3]

What concerned the U.S. steel industry and, to a certain extent, all non-China steelmakers, is that as China adds new and modernized steel capacity, it will be used increasingly to export surplus steel as domestic demand is met. Such concerns are exacerbated by stagnant steel demand in the United States, as the overall economy is still in a slow and fragile recovery from economic recession. Moreover, U.S. steelmakers have long alleged that Chinese steel and steel product exports are not only unfairly subsidized but also employ questionable, if not illegal, trade practices.

The issues for Congress include (1) whether China's steel capacity is being expanded beyond its domestic needs and being dumped on world markets; (2) whether Chinese control on exports of critical industrial inputs, such as rare earth metals, provides an unfair advantage to Chinese steelmakers and other manufacturers; (3) what actions, if any, should be taken to ensure that the Chinese currency exchange rate does not provide an unfair advantage to Chinese steel exporters; and (4) whether the U.S. government has sufficient resources allocated to combat attempts to evade trade duties, ensure the safety of imported products, and enforce U.S. trade laws.

OVERVIEW OF CHINA'S STEEL INDUSTRY

China's steel industry, along with a number of other key industries such as the automotive, textile, and petrochemical industries, is considered critical to the overall performance of the Chinese economy. The steel industry is considered a barometer of the overall economy. Similar to its automotive industry, China's steel industry is relatively young, with a humble beginning.

In 1949, the year the People's Republic of China was established, China's crude steel output was a negligible 158,000 tons. Chinese steel production then was highly concentrated in the northeast region, largely because of the Japanese influence and occupation before and during World War II. In the 1950s, with assistance from the former Soviet Union, which borders the northeast region of China, the Chinese government started to build steelmaking capacity. By 1957, China's annual steel production was over 5.3 million tons.[4]

After the political rift between China and the Soviet Union, which withdrew its assistance in 1961, the Chinese economy underwent further disruption during the Cultural Revolution (1966- 1976). Chinese steel development suffered a severe setback: steel output in 1970 was lower than in 1960.[5]

The Chinese economy went through stagnation, if not setbacks, during over two decades' interregnum from the time Mao came to power in the 1950s until his successor, Deng Xiaoping, began the economic reforms in the late 1970s. As the whole country opened up gradually to the world and adopted a more market-oriented approach, so did China's steel industry.

During the economic reforms, steelmakers not only began to adopt more advanced technology from foreign steel producers, but also started to welcome foreign investment and imports of raw materials. China's flagship steelmaker, now a major global producer, Shanghai Baosteel, was built in the late 1970s and early 1980s.[6] In 2009, Shanghai Baosteel was ranked the second-largest steel manufacturer in the world (see Table 1).

In the 1980s, China was a major importer of foreign steel, since its domestic steel production was not able to keep up with domestic demand. Many industrialized countries, back then, concluded that China's principal significance in the global steel market had been as a huge market for exported steel, as noted in *Steel and the State*, a book on the steel industry in the 1970s and 1980s by Thomas Howell, William Noellert, Jesse Kreier, and Alan Wolff:

> Chinese apparent consumption of crude steel in 1986 was 75.7 million metric tons, more than twice that of West Germany, but its production was only 51.9 million metric tons. The longstanding gap between Chinese production capability and demand has created the largest national export market in the world outside of the united States.... China has absorbed a substantial portion of the western world's surplus production.[7]

Table 1. World's Top Steel Companies, 2009

Global Rank	Company	HQ Country	2009 Output (mmt)
1	ArcelorMittal	Luxemburg	77.5
2	Baosteel	China	31.3
3	POSCO	South Korea	31.1
4	Nippon Steel	Japan	26.5
5	JFE Steel	Japan	25.8
6	Jiangsu Shagang	China	20.5
7	Tata Steel	India	20.5
8	Ansteel	China	20.1
9	Severstal	Russia	16.7
10	Evraz	Luxemburg	15.3
11	U.S. Steel	United States	15.2
12	Shougang	China	15.1
13	Gerdau	Brazil	14.2
14	Nucor	United States	14.0
15	Wuhan	China	13.7
16	Steel Authority of India Ltd.	India	13.5
17	Handan	China	12.0
18	Riva	Italy	11.3
19	Sumitomo	Japan	11.0
20	ThyssenKrupp	Germany	11.0

Source: World Steel Association, *World Steel in Figures 2010*, p.8.

By the end of the 1980s, the rapid growth of the Chinese economy led to a sharp increase in steel demand, and China's continuing dependency on imported steel became "one of the important factors restricting the development of the national economy."[8]

One principal objective of China's seventh five-year plan was to grow steel production to 60 million metric tons by the end of 1990, and to 80 million tons by 1995. In reality, China surpassed these goals, producing 61 million tons of crude steel in 1989, and 95 million tons in 1995.[9]

China Becomes Top Steel Producer and Consumer

In 1995, China's steel production reached 95 million metric tons (mmt), about the same amount produced by steelmakers in the United States that year. In 1996, Chinese steel output went beyond 101 mmt, passing the 100-mmt mark for the first time, as China overtook Japan to become the world's largest steel producer. China has held the title of the world's largest steel producer since 1996.

Figure 1 illustrates the speed and magnitude with which China has become the world's top steel producer, especially since 2000. In 2003, China produced 222 mmt of steel, more than United States' and Japan's combined output. In 2009, China produced about half of the world's steel, 10 times the U.S. production. One notable fact is, unlike most major steel-producing countries whose production was curtailed considerably due to the economic recession, Chinese steel output grew by 13.5% in 2009 from 500 mmt in 2008. In 2009, China accounted for about 46% of the world's total crude steel output, which represents a considerable increase from its share of 16% in 1999. This high production level was supported by China's domestic steel demand, spurred by strong economic growth during the first decade of the 21st century.

The World Steel Association (formerly known as the International Iron and Steel Institute), an industry association representing steel producers globally, compiled a list of major steel producers in annual steel output tonnage. Table 1 provides a list of the world's top 20 steel companies in 2009. It is worth noting that Chinese production rose sharply in 2009, while steel output in most industrialized countries declined. Table 2 lists the top 20 steel-producing countries. In 2009, China produced 567 mmt of steel, 10 times as much as the United States and over 6 times as much as the world's second-largest steel producer, Japan. Six Chinese steel companies were among the global top 20 steel producers in 2009.

In 2009, the Chinese GDP growth rate was about 9%, an impressive number as most of the developed countries were still mired by the global economic recession. Many believe that such strong growth was largely, if not entirely, fuelled by the central government's stimulus package, which has resulted in large amounts of outstanding bank loans, exposing banks to greater default risks. Further, it has been reported that the local Chinese governments (e.g., provincial, municipal, etc.) were likely to default on 20% of their stimulus bank loans, since many loans had been assigned to projects that were never meant to make large profits.[10] This, inevitably, raises the question whether China's rapid economic growth is sustainable.

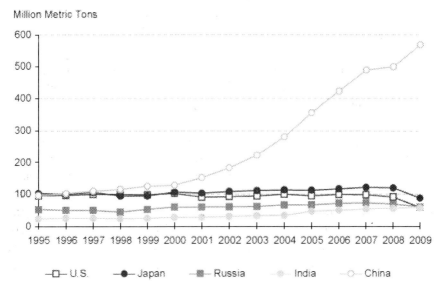

Source: World Steel Association.

Figure 1. Crude Steel Production, 1995-2009.

Although the central government, reportedly, has been trying to rein in its overheated economy in 2010, the steel production in China during the first half of 2010 did not slow down. According to World Steel Association statistics, China produced approximately 323 million metric tons of crude steel during the first half of 2010.

Table 2. Top Steel-Producing Countries, 2009

Rank	Country	Million Metric Tons of Crude Steel Production		
		2009	2008	% Change
1	China	567.8	500.3	13.5%
2	Japan	87.5	118.7	-26.3%
3	Russia	59.9	68.5	-12.6%
4	United States	58.1	91.4	-36.4%
5	India	56.6	55.1	2.7%
6	South Korea	48.6	53.6	-9.3%
7	Germany	32.7	45.8	-28.6%
8	Ukraine	29.8	37.3	-20.1%
9	Brazil	26.5	33.7	-21.4%
10	Turkey	25.3	26.8	-5.6%
11	Italy	19.8	30.6	-35.3%
12	Taiwan, China	15.9	19.9	-20.1%
13	Spain	14.4	18.6	-22.6%
14	Mexico	14.0	17.2	-18.6%
15	France	12.8	17.9	-28.5%
16	Iran	10.9	10.0	9.0%
17	United Kingdom	10.1	13.5	-25.2%
18	Canada	9.3	14.8	-37.2%
19	South Africa	7.5	8.3	-9.6%
20	Poland	7.1	9.7	-26.8%

Source: World Steel Association, *World Steel in Figures 2010*.

Steel Consumption and Capacity

During the course of China's rapid industrialization and urbanization, domestic demand for steel has increased. Commercial and residential construction, infrastructure building, and the rise in automobile sales, for example, all use significant amounts of steel. The major steel-consuming sectors in China are construction, automotive, shipbuilding, and home appliances.

Figure 2 illustrates the relationship between Chinese steel supply and demand between 1995 and 2009. As crude steel production continues to increase, especially from 2000, Chinese steel supply not only met domestic demand, but also began to outpace consumption.

According to the *Steel Statistics Yearbook* published by the World Steel Association, China imported more steel products (semi-finished and finished) than exported, which made it a net steel importer for decades, until 2005. In 2005, China became a net steel exporter, and has remained so in the years that followed.[11]

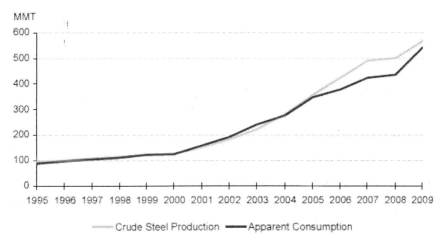

Source: World Steel Association, *World Steel in Figures*: 2005, 2008, 2010.

Figure 2. Chinese Steel Production and Consumption, 1995-2009.

As China's steel-producing capacity continued to increase, it did not take long to outpace the domestic consumption needs. This overcapacity problem became acute in 2006. By the end of 2008, China's steel capacity, reportedly, was 660 mmt, leaving approximately 160 mmt of excess supply.[12] This degree of excessive capacity has adversely affected the overall profitability of the steel industry—every time steel prices started to attain profitable levels, steel mills with idle capacity would increase output, resulting in downward pressure on steel product prices.

Nevertheless, there has been lingering caution, if not fear, that the global recovery is not likely to be swift or as strong as expected. China's economic growth has been moderating from the fast pace set at the beginning of 2010. The Chinese government, reportedly, has been trying to cool down the economy and engineer a soft economic landing. There are indications that Chinese property prices are easing and the growth of car sales is slowing. In order to cope with sluggish steel demand and to minimize losses from unprofitable sales, many Chinese mills have opted to curtail output and/or maintenance outage in the summer months of 2010.[13]

China's Steel Industry Structure and Composition

China's steel industry has its own unique composition and structure.

The Chinese steel industry, from iron and steel production to distribution channels and service centers, remains highly fragmented. According to a news analysis released on the official website of the Chinese government, there are reportedly about 1,200 steel manufacturers in China, albeit the exact count seems hard to confirm. Among these 1,200 steelmakers, about 70 are considered large or medium-sized producers.[14] The rest are small steel mills, many of which are not equipped with modern technology and often are inefficient and/or cause environmental problems.

Such a disaggregated structure, according to Chinese steel experts at China Iron & Steel Association, (CISA), has forced bigger steel manufacturers to expand production, often irrationally, to outweigh smaller competitors. Moreover, because steel companies tend to look after their own business interests, it has been difficult for large and small steel companies to form a united front and leverage bargaining power when negotiating price with international iron ore miners. The importance of iron ore supply and price will be discussed in further detail in a later section of this report.

Almost all major Chinese steel producers are state-owned, except Shagang Steel, which is the largest privately owned steel company in China. As a result, the company is not as vulnerable to foreign trade suits involving anti-dumping or government subsidies as some of the state-owned steel producers.

However, this does not imply that Shagang operates entirely in a market-oriented environment. According to World Steel Dynamics, an industry consulting and data services firm, even as a private enterprise, Shagang follows the guidelines that govern other Chinese steel companies: business expansion programs must be approved by the central and/or local government; the local government collects a portion of its value added taxes; and the top management personnel of Shagang are Communist Party members.[15]

Supply of Key Steel-Making Raw Materials

There are two main steel production technologies: integrated steelmaking, which uses the blast furnaces (BF) and basic oxygen furnaces (BOF), and the electric arc furnace (EAF).

An important technological characteristic of China's steel production is that crude steel is predominantly produced in blast furnaces and basic oxygen furnaces, which makes iron ore and coke critical raw materials to the steel industry in China. China produces sufficient coal and coke in this regard. However, when it comes to iron ore, China relies heavily on imports.

The production of steel in integrated mills uses the classic BF and BOF technology. Iron ore, the principal ingredient to produce pig iron in blast furnaces, is layered with coke and limestone. Hot air is blown into the furnace, igniting the coke and melting the iron ore. The molten iron is then processed into steel by eliminating impurities in the BOF and, possibly, adding alloying agents.

According to statistics released by World Steel Association, nearly 91% of the crude steel produced in China, by tonnage, comes from integrated mills, which use iron ore as primary charge.[16] Because domestic iron ore production in China, both in terms of quality and quantity, is not adequate to meet the growing steel industry demand, more than half of the iron ore has to be imported. This has put China in a sensitive, if not vulnerable, position with regard to iron ore supply and prices. On the other hand, the surging demand for iron ore and other raw materials by China also appears to have changed the world supply-demand relations.

Coal

Coke is one of the key raw materials in steelmaking. It is made by baking coal in an airless furnace or oven at high temperatures. As the primary reducing agent, coke reduces iron ore to molten iron.

As a major coal mining country, China is the world's leading supplier of coke. It remained a net exporter of coal until 2008, when the demand for coal to meet its energy and manufacturing needs outpaced the domestic supply. In 2009, China became a net importer of coal for the first time. It bought 104 million metric tons of coal, including both thermal coal (used to fire power plants) and coking coal.

This is not to suggest that the Chinese domestic coal production is insufficient. The reported Chinese annual output of coal was about 3.3 billion metric tons, the largest in the world. China's shift to coal imports indicates that as the nation continues its industrialization and urbanization efforts, the needs for energy and manufacturing resources have grown considerably and are likely to remain strong. Meanwhile, the shift also reflects, in part, a government-backed drive to consolidate the coal mining industry in China as well as to shut down illegal and unsafe mines. The consolidation drive started in Shanxi province, China's leading coal producing province whose output accounts for more than 20% of the country's total, and is moving to other big producing regions. Through consolidation, the Chinese government aims to improve coal industry structure and efficiency by eliminating tens of thousands of small local coal mines where outdated equipment, lax safety records, insufficient investment, and inefficient management have resulted in inefficient use of coal resources.[17]

China is not the only force driving up world coal demand. India's rising coal needs, along with those of South Korea, Taiwan, and possibly Vietnam in the near future, are contributing to the upturn in demand.

China and the Global Iron Ore Market

Iron ore is the world's second-largest commodity market by value, after only crude oil. The way iron ore is traded has a huge impact on the global economy because any changes in the cost of ore are passed through to the price of steel and then to consumer products from cars to washing machines. On the other hand, ore price is critical too, for the profitability of the world's major mining companies such as Rio Tinto and BHP Billiton and leading steelmakers such as ArcelorMittal and Baosteel.

The world iron ore industry has become very concentrated, dominated by the so-called "Big Three": Brazil's Vale is the largest producer with approximately 310 mmt of capacity in 2009, followed by two big Australian mining companies: Rio Tinto with 220 mmt of capacity and BHP Billiton with 140 mmt. Almost all of their production is exported, and the "Big Three" command about a 75% share of the seaborne trade market.[18] Therefore, the Big Three have controlling influence in determining global iron ore prices.

China, as the world's leading steel producer with ever-growing production capacity, feels it is crucial to secure iron ore supplies both globally and domestically, in order to plan, manage, and continue its industrial growth. China has become the major buyer of seaborne iron ore. Its ore imports have increased nearly eight times over the past decade, rising from about 70 mmt in 2000 to 628 mmt in 2009.[19] In 2000, China accounted for about 16% of global iron ore imports. In 2009, it bought nearly 70% of global supplies.[20]

Reportedly, China has an estimated 8,000 or more iron ore mines, but most of them are very small, and their production is not reliable. China has ramped up the domestic iron production in recent years. The total domestic iron ore output was about 180 mmt in 2009. However, small mines may be gradually closed during the 2010-2015 period, reducing the total production.[21]

Moreover, there exists a crucial constraint regarding iron ore production in China. Most of the Chinese domestic deposits are low grade hematite ores, with high impurities and a relatively low iron content between 30% and

35%.[22] Iron ore from Brazilian or Australian mines, by comparison, offers average iron content between 55% and 65%.[23]

Until steel prices declined sharply in late 2008, iron ore traded only in limited amounts in the open market. Its key prices were set by annual contract since the 1960s. Starting in the early 2000s, China's rapidly expanding steel production and its demand for higher-quality ores transformed iron ore into a commodity in high demand on the global market. As a result, the 40- year-old annual benchmark system began to shift.[24]

China started to play a leading role in the annual contract negotiations and set the price for 2008. In the 2009 negotiations, the Japanese steelmakers were the first to settle, accepting a 33% discount to the previous benchmark price with Rio Tinto in May 2009. Chinese steelmakers, represented by CISA (China Iron and Steel Association, representing 100 member companies), rejected the agreement and demanded a 45% price cut. China never agreed to a 2009-2010 contract price.[25]

The Rio Tinto Case

On June 5, 2009, Rio Tinto abandoned plans for a $19.5 billion capital investment from Chinalco, a Chinese state-owned miner which, reportedly, led to an embarrassment for the Chinese government. On July 5, 2009, the Chinese authorities detained four China-based Rio Tinto employees (dubbed the "Rio Four" by media), among whom three were Chinese nationals and the other was an Australian citizen with Chinese ethnicity. The Rio Four were accused of accepting bribes and stealing internal memos outlining China's negotiation plan. CISA accused them of undermining its position during the negotiations by revealing commercial secrets to Rio Tinto.[26]

In mid-July 2009, the Chinese authorities broadened a corruption investigation of its steel industry in connection to the Rio Four allegation. This led to questioning and detention of a few Chinese steel industry executives on alleged widespread bribery in business dealings. There were also allegations that the four Rio employees paid for detailed government trade and industry data, which gave Rio Tinto an edge in iron ore negotiations with Chinese state-owned steelmakers and subsequently derailed the process.[27] Two Chinese steel mill executives, reportedly, were charged with commercial espionage and bribery, fined, and sentenced to jail terms.[28]

In March 2010, nine months after the Rio Four were arrested, a Shanghai court sentenced them to between 7 and 14 years in prison for bribery and commercial secrecy violations. Media were barred from the courtroom and parts of the trial were held in secret. With speculation ranging widely on the

Chinese government's motivations in this case, the foreign business community inevitably questioned if the main impetus for the trial had been political.[29]

Despite the strains, Rio Tinto apparently moved to repair its relationship with China. In March 2010, Rio and Chinalco reached an agreement to jointly develop an iron ore project in the western African country of Guinea. Chinalco is the largest shareholder of Rio, and China is Rio's largest customer for iron ore, having bought $10.7 billion worth of iron ore in 2009 from Rio, which accounted for over 24% of Rio's sales.[30]

Iron Ore Trade Moves to Quarterly Prices

The Chinese steelmakers, represented jointly by Baosteel and CISA, never concluded their iron ore price negotiations with the Big Three for 2009. The Australian miners, nevertheless, continued to supply China with ore at the prices settled by the Japanese and South Korean steel producers.

As demand for iron ore (among other minerals and natural resources necessary to fuel industrial development) from China and other developing countries continues to increase, the importance of commodities seems to rise as well, both economically and geopolitically.

The gap between China's soaring demand and its domestic iron ore supply has made China increasingly dependent on imports. While the highly consolidated iron ore suppliers would like to retain control over supply and prices, the Chinese are becoming more adamant that they should have certain leverage as a major buyer. Meanwhile, the strong growth in demand, generated by China, has led to the emergence of a global spot market. In late 2008 and early 2009, it was the difference between iron ore spot and contract prices that led to a wave of defaults on annual contracts.[31]

Steelmakers then walked away from their annual contracts and bought iron ore at much lower prices on the spot market. Such disruptions, perhaps also aided by the Rio Four case as well as the strained business relations between Chinalco and Rio, eventually led to the collapse of the annual contract system. In April 2010, a new quarterly price system was introduced by the miners. It uses quarterly contracts, rather than the annual deals, and the cost is determined by an average of the spot market level instead of through bilateral and lengthy negotiations with major steelmakers.[32] The quarterly contracts, supposedly, will diminish the incentive for the steelmakers to default on annual iron ore contracts.

This new pricing system, which was put in place in April 2010, has survived its first quarterly test. But it is still to be tested under various conditions, for instance, with prices going up and going down. While many steel company executives reportedly prefer a return to annual pricing, both sides agree that the inevitable gap between spot and quarterly prices still means the system is under stress and that the way ore is traded is still to evolve.[33]

Although the implication of the movement (from annual contract price to the more volatile quarterly price) to the Chinese steelmakers remains to be seen, it will add uncertainties to the Chinese steel industry, which operates in an arguably market-oriented environment. To mitigate these uncertainties and to counter the market dominance of the Big Three suppliers, the Chinese steel producers are very likely to become more vertically integrated by aggressively seeking and/or acquiring new iron ore assets and suppliers.

In July 2010, *China Daily*, a newspaper backed by the Chinese central government, reported that Wuhan Iron & Steel Group, China's third-biggest steelmaker, would buy iron ore from Venezuela at a long-term contract. The deal was hailed as the encouraging "first-ever contract under the 'China Price' separate from rates set by Big Three."[34]

China's Quest for Iron Ore, among Other Natural Resources

With the central government's encouragement and approval, China's major iron and steel manufacturers have been actively seeking to secure supplies of raw materials. This wave of "going global" from China is not restricted to iron ore. The world has seen an increase in these activities since the global recession took place, which has weakened demand and kept the investment prices more reasonable. Another important factor is that many mining companies and resources-rich regions are looking for financial investments in a tightened credit market.

China has emerged as a big buyer and investor seeking energy and mining assets all around the world. According to data tracker Dealogic, companies based in China or Hong Kong participated in $13 billion of overseas mining acquisitions and investments in 2009, one-third of the value of all cross-border mining mergers and acquisitions. This was about 100 times the Chinese investment level in 2005. In 2009, Chinese firms accounted for nearly 40% of all mining deals with foreign investors in Australia, historically a major destination for Chinese mining investments. In Canada, a relatively newer attraction to Chinese buyers, the rate was about 25%.[35]

In May 2010, six of the world's biggest mining and steel companies joined in an exploration effort on an unprecedented scale in west Africa, where some of the world's richest deposits of iron ore are found. These groups are

Vale of Brazil; Rio Tinto and BHP Billiton of Australia; ArcelorMittal, the world's largest steelmaker; Russia's Severstal; and Chinalco, the state-owned Chinese mining company.[36]

The Chinese government has not made any explicit public push for overseas acquisitions. However, the government states clearly in its "Steel Industry Revitalization Plan" that it supports steel sector companies to further explore and develop domestic resources as well as to seek resources and invest abroad. Some support from the central government came in the form of state loans.[37] The acceleration of deals in recent years, many by state-owned enterprises, suggests that such acquisitions may be a priority.

Rare Earth Metals[38]

While China relies on foreign sources for iron ore, it has predominant control over the mining of the 17 rare earth elements (REEs). These 17 elements are essential for the manufacturing of many high-tech products from iPods to fiber-optic cables and military weapon systems. They are also important for the development of green technologies, such as wind turbines, and batteries for hybrid and electric cars.

China produces about 95% of the world's rare earth metals. The United States was once self-reliant on domestically produced REEs but has become dependent on imports, over 90% of which come from China, because of lower-cost operations. The concentration of production of REEs outside the United States has raised the important issue of supply vulnerability.

China has established domestic production quotas on REEs and has been cutting down export quotas for rare earth since 2005. It also increased export taxes to a range of 15% to 25%, indirectly raising prices for non-Chinese competitors. In July 2010, China announced that it would reduce its REE exports further in the second half of 2010 by 72%, the latest move to restrict exports of the metals.[39]

It appears that the aims of China's policy moves are not restricted to tight control over REE supply and prices. Similar to the encouragement from the Chinese government to promote exports of more value-added steel products, China seems determined to expand into the more profitable and sophisticated downstream REE processing sectors instead of just being world's supplier of raw materials. While accelerating the consolidation and restructuring of the fragmented REE mining industry, China has indicated that it expects foreign companies to set up rare earth processing plants in China in its so-called "technology for market" strategy.[40]

The U.S. Congress is increasingly concerned about access to rare earth raw materials and downstream products used in many national security applications as well as clean energy applications. Legislative proposals H.R. 4866 (Hoffman) and S. 3521 (Murkowski) have been introduced in the 111th Congress to address the issues and to support domestic production of REEs.

CHINA'S STEEL INDUSTRY POLICIES AND MEASURES

As the growth of steel production and capacity accelerated between 2000 and 2009, the Chinese government has acknowledged its growing concern over industry overcapacity, which has become acute since 2006. This has added growing pressure on domestic steel prices and subsequently, the profitability of steel companies.

The central government has been pushing provincial and municipal authorities to phase out obsolete capacity, usually by setting a target of total plant closures for the entire country and then disaggregating to regional targets.[41] The government also is keen on encouraging consolidations and technological upgrades, and improving the overall industry structure.

According to *China's Industrial Development Report 2009* by the Chinese Academy of Social Science, a state-backed think tank, China does not have sufficient natural resources and environmental capacity to be the world's steel supplier. Therefore, from a long-term perspective, the steel industry should focus on meeting domestic demand and never be export-driven. This may explain why export tax rebates on certain steel products were lowered or abolished by the Chinese government between 2007 and 2008, when export taxes were levied on certain export steel products.[42]

However, with the global steel demand, the priority for policy makers is to keep the Chinese steel industry stable. *China's Industrial Development Report 2009* stated that the Chinese steel industry should keep its share on the global market stable by making appropriate policy adjustments, using, for example, export quotas, export rebates, and increased export rebate rates on high value-added products, etc.[43]

The Steel Industry Revitalization Plan

In November 2008, the Chinese government unveiled its fiscal stimulus package worth RMB (¥) 4 trillion (U.S. $586 billion), to boost domestic demand and avert an economic slowdown amid the global economic downturn. In 2009, the government announced a program of incentives to promote vehicle sales and home appliance trade-ins, which are considered major steel-consuming sectors.

In spring 2009, the State Council, China's cabinet, issued a set of three-year industry revitalization plans. These three-year plans provide the latest blueprint for the key industries deemed critical to the overall health of the Chinese economy. The plans for the auto and steel industries are the first that were approved and publicly released by the central government.[44]

The Steel Industry Revitalization Plan (Steel Plan) was released on March 20, 2009. Some of the main objectives, as stated in the Steel Plan, are to modernize steel production through technical innovation and upgrades, control total output and eliminate obsolete capacity, improve industry structure and composition, and encourage global expansion while maintaining domestic market stability.[45]

The Steel Plan reiterates the goal to contain production at a proper level through production control and elimination of obsolete capacity. The central government, according to the plan, aims to reduce steel output to 460 million tons in 2009, 8% lower than 2008, and to gradually increase production to 500 million tons in 2011.

However, China's reported steel production in 2009 was over 567 million tons, already 23% over the planned 460 million tons, and already surpassing the production goal for 2011. This obvious disconnect between the planned and real steel output raises the question about how realistic or believable these planned targets are.

In early 2010, aiming to shut down small and inefficient steel mills, the Chinese government ordered the closure of blast furnaces smaller than 400 cubic meters as well as converters and electric-arc furnaces under 30 metric tons. It is also reported that the central government plans to shut down 6 mmt of outdated steel capacity and 25 mmt of iron capacity in 2010.[46]

In June 2010, facing a stagnant global steel market and a gradually cooling domestic economy, the Chinese government pushed ahead and ordered more steel capacity be closed by the end of September 2010. The government increased the previously planned 6 mmt of outdated steel capacity to 8.25 mmt and 25 mmt of iron capacity to 30.[47] It was also reported that some 40% of CISA's 77 member mills adopted maintenance outages in July 2010 to reduce output after domestic steel prices dropped below production costs. Several major Chinese steel mills, reportedly, would extend maintenance closures into August to manage output and minimize losses."[48]

It appears that the central government is committed to restraining steel capacity growth. However, it may not be easy to strike a balance between curtailing steel capacity and maintaining an optimal industry growth. There is little certainty that steel capacity cuts will be in pace with the decline in Chinese domestic steel demand. Therefore, if and when these policy measures will bring effective and meaningful solutions to China's over-capacity problem remains to be seen.

The Steel Plan strongly encourages the industry to rapidly improve technology levels in steelmaking and become more environmentally friendly, in order to improve efficiency, reduce production costs, improve product quality, and optimize product offering structure.

The Chinese government calls for mergers and acquisitions among steelmakers and increases in the industry concentration rate. The goal is to have the top five steelmakers holding 45% of Chinese steel output. It names Baosteel Group Corp., Angang Steel Co. Ltd., and Wuhan Iron & Steel (Group) Corp. as the leading steelmakers capable of global competition.

The Steel Plan even provides guidance for the geographical location of steel production in China. One of the main objectives is to grow coastal and riverside steel manufacturers so that they would constitute 40% of national output. To reduce industrial pollution, the Steel Plan announces that steel companies in a few major cities would be relocated.[49]

The central government calls for the steel industry to preserve the stability of iron ore imports and maintain market order. It also encourages steel manufacturers to further explore and develop local resources while supporting major enterprises that seek resources and investment opportunities abroad.

State Council Facilitates Industry Consolidation and Environmental Improvement[50]

On June 4, 2010, China's State Council issued a circular to expedite industry consolidation and improve environmental performance in the Chinese steel sector. It reiterated the key components stated in the revitalization plan, and also introduced or updated some policy measures. A few key points include:

1) Rein in steel capacity expansion—There will be no more approval for new capacity expansion projects until the end of 2011; any obsolete capacity that has been shut down shall not be replaced.

2) Expedite capacity closures—Incentives and punitive measures, such as higher electricity prices, will be used to speed up closure of obsolete capacities; the Ministry of Industry and Information Technology (MIIT) will release a list of steel facilities to be forcibly closed.
3) Facilitate industry consolidation—The production share of the top 10 steel companies is expected to reach 60% by 2015 from 44% in 2009; provincial governments are asked to have a consolidation plan at the regional level to be implemented in 2010-2011, with supporting measures including land access and financial resources to be adjusted accordingly.
4) Improve environmental performance by promoting environmentally sound technologies and practices; increase EAF-based steelmaking and improve recycling rate of scrap. As a measure to encourage more efficient use of technology and raw materials, Chinese trade policy will be adjusted accordingly to curb the export of low value-added steel products.
5) Support investment in technological advancement and product development, especially projects by key steel manufacturers.
6) Regulate iron ore import activities and increase concentration of Chinese importers. Secure stable ore supply and keep ore price at reasonable level by increasing domestic output while supporting steelmakers' investment in overseas mines.

It is notable that the circular listed trade policy adjustment under the objective of environmental improvement. This trade policy adjustment was issued in June 2010.

Tax Rebate Adjustment for Steel Products

On June 22, 2010, the Chinese Ministry of Finance and State Administration of Taxation jointly issued certain adjustment of steel export tax rebates. This removed the export tax rebate for key commodities, including some steel exports, effective July 15, 2010. Some believe the move was designed to ease tension with trading partners in the United States and the European Union, who have expressed increasing concern over China's steel export subsidies. It could also help to curb production overcapacity and speed up steel industry consolidation and restructuring, which the central government has tried unsuccessfully for years to achieve.[51]

The adjustment covers 406 products, non-ferrous metals, fertilizers, glass goods, and chemicals, etc. The existing 9% tax rebates are to be abolished for 48 steel products, including some heavy steel sections, plates, hot rolled coil, narrow strips, and coated products, etc. However, tax rebates for most of the high value-added products, such as steel pipes, cold rolled coil, and specialty steel, remain unchanged.[52]

This is the first tax rebate adjustment for Chinese steel exports since 2009. From April 2009, tax rebates of some high value-added steel products, such as cold rolled steel, alloy steel, and specialty steel, had been raised to 13%. In June 2009, export tax rebates for some other steel products were increased from a range between 0% and 5% to 9%. These products included heavy sections, hot rolled coil, sheet, plant, narrow strips, most alloy steels, railway products, ductile pipes, a few seamless and welded pipes, and some steel-structured products.[53]

Reportedly, the removal of export rebates and weaker steel demand did drive China's steel exports down in July 2010. Finished steel exports from China totaled 4.55 million tons in July, a 19% decrease from June 2010.[54] However, it remains to be seen whether the Chinese steel output will remain under control in the long term, especially when market conditions improve as the global economic recovery picks up speed.

The bottom line, it appears, is that the rebate rollbacks will cut exports of mostly low-end commodity-grade products. The effect will put more pressure on Chinese domestic steel producers and help the central government's goal of closing older and polluting steel mills.

IMPLICATIONS FOR THE U.S. STEEL INDUSTRY: ISSUES FOR CONGRESS

Chinese steel is used mainly in its domestic market. What has concerned the U.S. steel industry is that, as China adds new and modernized steel capacity, it will be used increasingly to export surplus steel after domestic demand is adequately met. When China hits a period of overproduction and surpluses, a natural reaction would be to export the excess steel.

Steelmakers in the United States believe that China's steel industry subsidization by its government (in the form of an undervalued currency;

export rebates and/or quotas; subsidized financing; and relatively weak environmental, labor, and safety regulations) is one of the key issues affecting the health of U.S. steel sector. There have been multiple anti-dumping and countervailing cases in the United States against Chinese steel products, suggesting that U.S. steel producers and trade officials are increasingly using trade remedies to enforce international trade laws.

In June 2010, China responded to heavy pressure by the United States and other members of the G20 major economies by announcing a more flexible currency standard. China's decision to drop the two-year-old informal peg to the U.S. dollar was welcomed by the United States and other trading partners.[55] But with the government's insistence on gradual change, the timing and the magnitude of the Chinese currency appreciation and, subsequently, any meaningfully positive impact on the U.S. (and the global) steel market still remains unclear.

Chinese Steel Capacity and Exports

China has been on course to modernize steel production through streamlining the steel sector via closures and consolidation. As mentioned in previous sections, the Chinese steel sector still faces the challenge of over-supply and over-capacity, despite the commitment and efforts of its central government to tackle the problems.

However, Chinese steel production does not appear to be export-driven. In other words, the majority of Chinese steel has been used to supply domestic economic growth. In 2009, largely spurred by strong domestic demand, China's exports fell about 60% from the previous year to 23 million tons, dropping its ranking as the top exporter in 2008. In 2009, Chinese steel exports by tonnage were behind Japan, the European Union, Russia, and Ukraine.[56] China's reported steel imports in 2009 reached 22 million tons, making the country the world's largest importer.[57]

Figure 3 is based on the annual steel statistics released by the World Steel Association. It shows that the Chinese steel industry, along with those of India and the United States, is one of the three major national producers least dependent on exports. In the case of China, steel exports in 2009 were 4% of output, while in India they were less than 10%, and in the United States they were nearly 16%. Three leading Asian producers outside China (Japan, South Korea, and Taiwan) had export ratios as high as 38%, 41%, and 62% of their respective production in 2009. Russia and Canada exported about half of their output, Germany 63.5%, and Ukraine over 80%.

Between 2005 and 2009, China's steel exports as a percent of total production were between 4.2% and 13.5%, similar to those of the United States, which were between 10% and 16%.

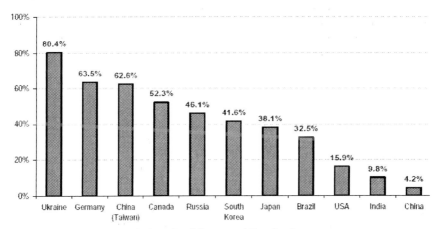

Source: World Steel Association, *Steel Statistical Yearbook*.

Figure 3. Steel Exports by Country, 2009; As a Percent of Total Output.

In terms of total steel mill products imported into the United States, by tonnage, over 30% came from the NAFTA countries (Canada and Mexico). In 2009, Canada and Mexico accounted for over 36% of the total tonnage of steel mill products imported into the United States, the European Union accounted for 16%, and China accounted for 9%, followed by South Korea's 8.2% and Japan's 7.5%. From 2005 to 2009, the Chinese share of total U.S. steel mill products imports has been between 7% (in 2005) and 15% (in 2008).[58]

Even though steel industry statistics seem to agree with China's position that it has little intention of creating an export-oriented steel industry, the potential exists that with China accounting for nearly half of global output, marginal shifts by its steel industry in the direction of increased exports may lead to considerable market disruptions for other suppliers. As global steel demand remains sluggish in 2009 and into the first half of 2010, and Chinese economic growth slows down, the concern of U.S. steelmakers is that the U.S. market may see an increase in steel imports from China.

Steel Trade Development

Steelmakers in the United Stated have long claimed that Chinese steel and steel products are unfairly subsidized by its government. According to Steel Market Intelligence (SMI), a steel industry consultancy, and a Eurofer (European Steel Trade Association) report cited in SMI's newsletter, China supports its steel industry with a variety of mechanisms including grants, capital market interventions, preferential taxes, subsidized loans, access to below-market priced inputs, and nominal labor and environmental protection, among other mechanisms.[59]

Chinese steel exports are assisted, SMI says, by an "intricate set of cascading value added tax rebates, export taxes, and even export quotas on inputs, plus tax cuts, export credits and other schemes provided by the Chinese state-owned financial institutions."[60]

Anti-Dumping and Countervailing Case Against Chinese OCTG Imports[61]

On April 8, 2009, seven U.S. Oil Country Tubular Goods (OCTG) producers and the United Steelworkers Union (USW) filed complaints against Chinese OCTG imports, alleging that Chinese pipe has been illegally dumped and subsidized by the Chinese government, and therefore, has materially harmed domestic producers. This marks the biggest steel trade case brought against China before the U.S. International Trade Commission (USITC) to date, and is valued at about $2.8 billion of subsidized Chinese steel.

Preliminary determinations by both the USITC and the U.S. Department of Commerce (USDOC) have ruled in favor of the U.S. producers in the countervailing case, saying that Chinese producers received subsidies, and placed countervailing duties ranging from 10.9% to 30.7%.

On November 24, the USDOC made its final determination on the countervailing case, lowering the average duties placed on Chinese producers to a range of 10% to 16%. On December 30, 2009, USITC issued a final ruling in favor of the U.S. domestic petitioners, affirming countervailing duties from 10% to 16%.

Meanwhile, the USITC and the USDOC also ruled in favor of the U.S. producers in the antidumping investigations, stating the Chinese companies were selling below fair market value. On May 4, 2010, following Commerce's April 9 final decision, the USITC issued its affirmative determinations, upholding antidumping duties ranging from 30% to 99%, which were placed on the OCTG imports from China.

The ruling of this high-profile trade case was welcomed and praised by the U.S. steel producers.

The USW president, Leo Gerard, as quoted in *American Metal Market (AMM)*, said that the ITC vote "makes it clear to American pipe workers and industry that the U.S. government will stand up against China's violation of fair trade rules when domestic job losses and industry injury are clearly demonstrated."[62]

Anti-Dumping and Countervailing Complaints Against Other Chinese Steel Product Imports

In 2009 and 2010, trade petitions against Chinese steel product imports have increased considerably. The U.S. Commerce Department and the USITC have separately granted a number of requests to impose tariffs on various categories of imports from China, after finding evidence that these products were subsidized and/or dumped in the U.S. market.

These subsidized and/or dumped Chinese steel imports include drill pipe,[63] certain seamless carbon and alloy steel standard, line, and pressure pipe,[64] steel grating,[65] and steel wire strand for pre-stressed concrete (PC wire strand).[66]

In another anti-dumping and countervailing case against wire decking imports from China, the USITC ruled in favor of the Chinese producers. It determined that the U.S. producers of wire decking were neither materially injured nor threatened with material injury by Chinese imports, and therefore imposed no anti-dumping or countervailing duty orders. This was the first steel product trade case of 2010 that went in favor of foreign producers or importers.[67]

In August 2010, The U.S. domestic wire decking producers filed an appeal with the U.S. Court of International Trade (USCIT) in August 2010, challenging the July 1 decision by the USITC that unfairly traded imports of the product from China were not injuring U.S. manufacturers. The final ruling is pending.[68]

Chinese Steel Plate Faces Anti-Dumping Circumvention Inquiry[69]

On February 17, 2010, four major U.S. producers of carbon steel plate products asked the U.S. Department of Commerce to prevent another Chinese company from adding boron to steel plate in an alleged attempt to circumvent anti-dumping orders.

The domestic plate manufacturers accused Chinese producer Wuyang Iron & Steel Co. Ltd. and importer Stemcor USA Inc. of importing cut-to-length plate products containing metallurgically insignificant amounts of boron in order to classify the plate as alloy product, which would be outside the scope of the anti-dumping order against certain cut-to-length carbon steel plate from China. It is alleged that the plate contains 0.0008% or more boron by weight.

On April 23, 2010, the USDOC initiated an anti-dumping circumvention inquiry based on the complaints from the U.S. producers. Commerce, according to a notice in the *Federal Register*, intends to issue a final determination within 300 days of the initiation notice.

In a similar case filed in 2008 involving two Chinese trading companies adding boron to steel so as to circumvent a U.S. anti-dumping order, Commerce issued a final determination in 2009 in favor of the U.S. producers.[70]

China's Export Restriction of Certain Industrial Raw Materials

On November 4, 2009, the United States, the European Union, and Mexico jointly made a formal request to the WTO for a dispute settlement panel to address China's export restrictions on raw materials.[71] The Chinese export restraints on numerous raw materials, allegedly, "significantly distort the international market and provide preferential conditions for Chinese industries that use these raw materials." The raw materials at issue are bauxite, coke, fluorspar, magnesium, manganese, silicon metal, silicon carbide, yellow phosphorus, and zinc, which are used by the steel, aluminum, automotive, and chemicals industries.[72]

China, allegedly, imposes quotas on exports of bauxite, coke, fluorspar, silicon carbide, and zinc, as well as certain intermediate products incorporating some of these inputs. It also levies export duties on several raw materials and imposes other export restrictions through its export procedures.[73] The United States charges that such industrial policies are intended to lower raw material prices for Chinese manufacturers, especially in the steel, aluminum, and chemicals sectors, in order to help them obtain an unfair competitive advantage.

The WTO's biennial trade policy review for China, which was released in June 2010, suggested that the WTO was not entirely satisfied with the application of China's resource export controls, stating that "export restraints for whatever reason tend to reduce export volumes of the targeted products and divert supplies to the domestic market, leading to a downward pressure on the domestic pieces of these products. The resulting gap between domestic prices and world prices constitute implicit assistance to domestic downstream processors of the targeted products and thus provides them a competitive advantage."[74]

China claims that these measures are intended to conserve exhaustible natural resources and protect the environment. The final ruling on this WTO case is still pending.

Chinese Direct Steel Investment in the United States

China has been seeking to curb its steel overcapacity while maintaining stabilized growth. At home, the government appears to have expedited efforts to consolidate and restructure the industry. Overseas, it has encouraged steel producers to acquire and invest in mining, energy, and manufacturing sectors. While the majority of industrialized countries, including the United States, are slowly recovering from the economic downturn, such moves from Chinese companies could face challenges and resistance from the targeted company and/or its host country.

A proposed joint venture between one of China's leading steel producers and a U.S. steel company has drawn deep concerns from the U.S. steel industry as well as lawmakers.

In May 2010, China's Anshan Iron & Steel Group Corp. (Anshan, also known as AnSteel), a major state-owned steel manufacturer, announced its plan to invest in an Amory, Mississippi-based U.S. steel mill, Steel Development Corp. (SDCO). Anshan agreed to provide financial investment and to build five mini-mills in the United States, four of them to produce reinforcing bars and a fifth to make flat-rolled steel products. The Chinese producer said that it would like to gain insight into electric furnace technology, to obtain experience in lowering energy consumption, and to curb dependence on imported iron ore.[75]

This infusion of investment capital from China has sparked controversy in the United States. The Steel Manufacturers Association (SMA) and the American Iron & Steel Institute (AISI) called on federal regulators to carefully examine the investment plan, raising concerns about the Chinese government financing in steel capacity and the lack of reciprocity that would allow a U.S. steel company to build similar manufacturing facilities in China.[76]

On July 2, 2010, 50 members of the U.S. Congressional Steel Caucus wrote to Treasury Secretary Tim Geithner, urging that Anshan's joint-venture plan should be thoroughly investigated by the Committee on Foreign

Investment in the U.S (CFIUS). CFIUS, the inter-agency committee headed by the Treasury secretary, formally conducts classified reviews of foreign takeovers of U.S. assets on security grounds and can recommend that the U.S. President block a transaction.

The caucus describes the proposed deal as a threat to "economic security," stating in the letter that the investment by a state-controlled Chinese company provides several unfair trade advantages to both the Chinese and to SDCO, and that it will eventually lead to the loss of American manufacturing jobs and the further migration of the U.S. manufacturing base. Worse, according to the Steel Caucus, the joint venture could give China "access to new steel production technologies and information regarding American national security infrastructure projects."[77]

Debates over "economic security" are often built on the argument that U.S. companies cannot compete against foreign state-owned entities in the U.S. market that are viewed as having a limitless check book. In 2005, China National Offshore Oil Co. (CNOOC) launched an $18.5 billion bid for Unocal, a California oil company. CNOOC withdrew the offer after strong opposition from U.S. lawmakers for fear that CNOOC had an unfair advantage. Soon after, Unocal was acquired by Chevron, the U.S. oil company.[78]

Secretary Geithner responded 10 days later to the Anshan-SDCO complaint, telling the Steel Caucus that Treasury was "aware of the proposed transaction" but promising no action. Considering the response inadequate and disappointing, the Steel Caucus wrote a letter to the White House seeking a federal investigation of the deal.[79]

In August 2010, Anshan confirmed it was committed to pushing forward the planned joint venture, after an executive of its subsidiary said the deal was on hold due to opposition from U.S. lawmakers.[80] In September 2010, Anshan and SDCO finalized a joint-venture agreement, under which Anshan will become a 14% partner of SDCO and join its board of directors.[81]

However, not all Chinese direct investment in the steel sector has faced such disapproval from the U.S. industry or regulators.

Chinese oil country tubular goods producer Tianjin Pipe (Group) Corp. (TPCO) plans to build a $1 billion greenfield pipe mill in San Patricio County, Texas. The mill is set to employ about 600 people. TPCO's investment has been welcomed by local development officials and building trades unions. Despite opposition by the United Steelworkers union, the mill received crucial regulatory approval in April 2010, and does not seem to have experienced the same political pressure that Anshan has been facing.[82]

Although the ultimate outcome of the Anshan-SDCO deal remains unclear at this point, it is likely that the world will see more Chinese investment in the near future. Anshan, along with other Chinese manufacturers, is reacting to domestic and international pressure for Chinese steel mills to control output and to look overseas for growth opportunities. If Chinese currency, the renminbi, were to appreciate further, such overseas investments would become more attractive to Chinese business enterprises.[83]

CONGRESSIONAL AND LEGISLATIVE REACTION

Introduction of S. 3725: The Enforcing Orders and Reducing Circumvention and Evasion Act of 2010

On August 5, 2010, Senators Wyden and Snowe introduced the Enforcing Orders and Reducing Circumvention and Evasion Act of 2010 (the Enforce Act), S. 3725, which would provide the U.S. Commerce Department tools to improve enforcement of U.S. trade laws.

The legislation states that exporters from developing countries, in particular China, have been known to mislabel shipments and re-route goods through third-party countries in an attempt to mislead customs officials and to circumvent U.S. trade laws.

The Senators, along with nine colleagues, also sent a letter to the White House urging the Obama Administration to do more to combat unfair trade practices. In the letter, the Senators called on the Administration to address China's alleged practice of currency manipulation, among other illegal trade practices.[84]

The Enforce Act is designed to combat the evasion of anti-dumping and countervailing duty orders and enforce existing trade remedy statutes, by empowering the U.S. Commerce Department to investigate trade remedy laws violations, establishing a rapid-response timeline by which Commerce and U.S. Customs would respond to allegations, and improving the safety of imports.

U.S. Trade Law Proposal[85]

On August 26, 2010, U.S. Commerce Secretary Gary Locke announced 14 proposed measures focused on illegal import practices from non-market economies. These steps aim to continue the rigorous enforcement of U.S. trade laws.

Some of the proposed changes:

- Currently, foreign companies can be excused from anti-dumping (AD) and countervailing duties (CVD) by demonstrating that they were not dumping or receiving subsidies for a certain period of time. Under the proposed change, such companies could be removed from the process only upon the normal countrywide expiration of those duties.
- Currently, once an initial affirmative determination is made in an AD/CVD case, importers are able to post a bond in the amount of the estimated duties owned. A new proposed measure will require importers to post cash deposits rather than bonds to facilitate entry of their goods and services into the United States.

Some other proposed changes would include improved methodology for determining the value of labor in non-market economy cases; tightening the certification process for the information submitted to Commerce as part of the AD/CVD case process; and strengthening specific rules to ensure that parties are paying the full amount of their duties.

Steel and metals industries have long been pushing for stricter trade laws enforcement, especially with regard to what has been referred to as China's mercantilist trade policies. Industry leaders and groups widely welcomed the new proposals, but some also maintained that China's allegedly illegal currency manipulation as a key trade distorting practice, which is not included in the proposed measures, still must be addressed.[86]

USW Files Trade Case with USTR[87]

On September 9, 2010, the United Steelworkers Union (USW) filed a comprehensive trade case with the U.S. Trade Representative (USTR), alleging that China has violated rules by subsidizing exports of clean energy equipment. The case is filed under Section 301 of the 1974 Trade Act, which sets an initial deadline of 45 days for the Administration to respond.[88]

The filing of this petition comes at a time of increasing trade and currency frictions with China. It asks the Obama Administration to begin formal proceedings at the World Trade Organization (WTO) to force China to repeal the subsidies.

The petition contends that the Chinese central and provincial governments have used land grants, low-cost loans and a number of other measures to help Chinese companies expand their share of the world market for clean energy equipment, at the expense of jobs in the United States and other parts of the world.

Besides Chinese government assistance to clean energy exporters, the USW petition accuses the Chinese government of breaking WTO rules by tightly restricting the exports of rare earth elements and by forcing foreign clean energy companies to license their technology to local partners as a condition of entry to the Chinese market. These issues have been discussed in a previous section in this report.

CONCLUSION

China's emergence as the world's largest steel producer and major manufacturing base has multiple ramifications to the United States and other countries. Its rapid growth in steel production requires an adequate and steady supply of raw materials. This means China will continue to have substantial influence over the global supply and price of raw materials and, indirectly, affect the production costs and profitability of its competitors.

Meanwhile, China's steel sector, with its own restrictions, may not continue the production capacity growth at the current rate. Lack of control over the supply and price of iron ore has been a major constraint. Other restrictions could be lackluster domestic demand caused by a slowing economy, high energy costs, and environmental implications.

China has been seeking and securing natural resources all over the globe to support its industrialization and urbanization efforts. At the same time, the Chinese government has put export restrictions on rare earth elements exports and other raw materials critical to industrial production. This suggests that the Chinese government prefers to grant its own manufacturers a competitive edge over foreign producers.

When China manages to assert more control over production inputs, the Chinese steel industry may be poised to significantly expand its share of the global production as well as the export market. Strict and timely enforcement of trade laws is important and helpful to the U.S. steel sector, when handling trade cases, albeit reactive. Adaptation of a consistent and long-term strategy is likely to serve the interest of the U.S. steel industry.

End Notes

[1] World Steel Dynamics, Chinese Steel Hits the Great Wall, Core Report H (May 2009), p. 13.
[2] Ibid.
[3] Financial Times, "All eyes on Beijing to drive world growth," July 12, 2010.
[4] Institute of Industrial Economies, Chinese Academy of Social Science (CASS), China's Industrial Development Report 2009 (Beijing, China: Economy & Management Publishing House, Sept. 2009 ed.), p. 248.
[5] Howell, Noellert, Kreier, and Wolff, Steel and the State, Economic Competition Among Nations Series (Boulder, CO: Westview Press, 1988 ed.), p. 367; Institute of Industrial Economies, Chinese Academy of Social Science (CASS), China's Industrial Development Report 2009 (Beijing, China: Economy & Management Publishing House, Sept. 2009 ed.), p. 251.
[6] Baosteel corporate website (http://www.baosteel.com/group_e/02about/ ShowArticle.asp?ArticleID=1384), as viewed on March 22, 2010; "About Baosteel Group Co.," a presentation prepared by Baosteel Co. Construction of Baosteel (also known as Baoshan Steel, and Baoshan Iron & Steel Co.) started in December 1978. The first phase of the project was completed in 1985 for steel production; the second stage in 1991; and the third in 2000. Japanese and West German steel companies participated in the early stage, as mentioned in Jim Mann's book, Beijing Jeep: A Case of Western Business in China (Boulder, CO: Westview Press, 1977 ed.), p. 66.
[7] Howell, Noellert, Kreier, and Wolff, Steel and the State, Economic Competition Among Nations Series (Boulder, CO: Westview Press, 1988 ed.), p. 366.
[8] Ibid.
[9] International Iron and Steel Institute (now World Steel Association), World Steel in Figures 1990, p. 3.
[10] Financial Times, "China banks resigned to defaults" (July 28, 2010).
[11] According to Steel Statistics Year Book released by World Steel Association: China was a net exporter of steel products from 2005 to 2009. This was also the case for the first quarter of 2010. Available data for first quarter of 2010, released by World Steel Association, suggests that China exported 23.28 million metric tons (mmt) of semi-finished and finished steel product, while importing 8.735 mmt.
[12] "Analysis: Containing steel production capacity is fundamental to the healthy growth of China's steel industry" (March 21, 2009) on the official website of The Central People's Government of the People's Republic of China, http://www.gov.cn/jrzg/2009-03/21/content_1264845.htm, as viewed on July 21, 2010. The author of this CRS report used the original Chinese-language version of the document.
[13] American Metal Market (AMM), "Chinese mills extend output cuts into Aug." (August 3, 2010).
[14] "Analysis: To revitalize the steel industry, China must increase industry concentration rate" (March 21, 2009) on the official website of The Central People's Government of the People's republic of China, http://www.gov.cn/jrzg/2009- 03/21/content_1264930.htm, as viewed on July 20, 2010. The author of this CRS report used the original Chinese-language version of the document.
[15] World Steel Dynamics, "Shagang Steel: World Class Steelmaker" (November 11, 2009).
[16] World Steel Association, Steel Statistical Yearbook 2009, Table 7. Approximately 42% of crude steel produced in the U.S. come from BF / BOF; Germany, 68%; Japan, 75%; South Korea, 56%; India, 40%.

[17] Financial Times, "Commodities: A market re-emerges" (April 13, 2010).
[18] World Steel Dynamics, North American Iron Ore: Consolidated Survival, p. 97.
[19] World Steel Dynamics, North American Iron Ore: Consolidated Survival, p. 45.
[20] Financial Times, "Ore struck" (April 6, 2010).
[21] Ibid., p. 99.
[22] Ibid. Hematite ores are generally hard to upgrade so they are often blended heavily with high-grade ores to provide good productivity for the blast furnace.
[23] U.S. Geological Survey, Mineral Commodity Summaries (January 2010).
[24] The U.S. steel industry is only indirectly affected by international iron ore supply and price developments. First, nearly 60% of steel in the U.S., by tonnage, is produced in electric arc furnaces (EAFs), which use ferrous scrap as primary charge. Second, in general, the U.S. integrated mills are supplied by major domestic iron ore producers in Michigan and Minnesota, as well as the eastern Canadian producers. Half of the iron ore capacity in North America is captively owned by two major steel companies, U.S. Steel and ArcelorMittal. According to U.S. Geological Survey, U.S. resources are mainly low-grade taconite type of ores from the Great lakes area, where three-quarters of the North American integrated mills are located. This proximity in location gives the major domestic iron ore producers an advantage over seaborne imports.
[25] Ibid.; Financial Times, "China rejects deal on iron ore price cuts" (May 31, 2009).
[26] Ibid. ; American Metal Market (AMM), "China has 'conclusive' proof of spying by Rio Tinto execs" (July, 2009); AMM, "Rio 'spying' case ensnares steel exec" (July 9, 2009); Financial Times, "Rio Executive held by China on suspicion of spying" (July 8, 2009); Bloomberg.com, "China detains Rio executive on suspicion of espionage" (July 8, 2009); New York Times, "China spy case linked to mining price dispute" (July 11, 2009).
[27] Financial Times, "China detains local executive as steel espionage probe widens" (July 10, 2009); Financial Times, "Rio dispute in China widens with bribe claim" (July 16, 2009); New York Times, "China broadens investigation of steel industry" (July 14, 2009).
[28] AMM, "Mill execs to face charges in Rio case" (March 8, 2010); AMM, "Shougang exec eyes sentence appeal" (August 6, 2010).
[29] Financial Times, "Rio Tinto courts China as bribery trial begins" (March 22, 2010); Financial Times, "Rio sacks staff jailed by China for bribery" (March 29, 2010); Bloomberg.com, "Rio Tinto iron ore workers face Shanghai Trial today" (March 21, 2010); Wall Street Journal, "Rio Tinto appeal rejected" (May 18, 2010).
[30] Ibid.; New York Times, "Rio Tinto and Chinalco in Deal for Iron Project" (March 19, 2010).
[31] For more details on the earlier price negotiations, see CRS Report R40541, The Fall in Steel and Other Metals Prices: Issues for Congress, by Rachel Tang.
[32] AMM, "CISA admits defeat in benchmark row" (April 29, 2010); Financial Times, "Annual iron ore contract system collapses" (March 30, 2010).
[33] AMM, "Global iron ore trends spark concern" (May 11, 2010); AMM, "ArcelorMittal mulling 'model' switch to quarterly steel contracts" (May 12, 2010); Financial Times, "Iron Ore's quarterly pricing system passes first hurdle" (August 5, 2010).
[34] "Wuhan Iron & Steel snaps up Venezuelan ore" on the China Daily website, http://www.chinadaily.com.cn/m/hubei/ 2010-07/22/content_11037664.htm, as viewed on August 10, 2010.
[35] Wall Street Journal, "Chinese firms snap up mining assets" (July 20, 2010).
[36] Financial Times, "Mining groups target west Africa" (May 18, 2010).
[37] Financial Times, "PetroChina secure $30bn state lean to fund 'go global' strategy." (September 10, 2009). China Development Bank, reportedly, provided a five-year loan at discounted

interest rate to fund PetroChina. The loan underlines the critical role that China Development Bank has been playing in the overseas expansions by Chinese companies. In 2009 it helped financed a $25bn loans-for-oil supply deal with Russia and a similar $10bn deal with Brazil. The bank also led the $21bn syndicate of Chinese banks that backed Chinalco's failed bid for a Rio Tinto stake, which is mentioned earlier in this report.

[38] There are 17 rare earth elements, 15 within the chemical group called lanthanides, plus yttrium and scandium. For more details on rare earth metals, their supply issues, and the legislative activities, see CRS Report R41347, Rare Earth Elements: The Global Supply Chain, by Marc Humphries.

[39] Bloomberg.com, "China 'power' over metals for smart bombs prompts U.S. hearing" (April 15, 2010); AMM, "China's new are earths quota increases US supply concerns" (July 26, 2010); "China reduces rare earth export quota by 72%" on the China Daily website, http://www.chinadaily.com.cn/bizchina/2010-07/09/content_10088082.htm, as viewed on August 16, 2010.

[40] Wall Street Journal, "China dangles rare-earth resources in investors" (August 16, 2010).

[41] World Steel Association, "The Chinese steel industry: a monthly update for Worldsteel members."

[42] Institute of Industrial Economies, Chinese Academy of Social Science (CASS), China's Industrial Development Report 2009 (Beijing, China: Economy & Management Publishing House, Sept. 2009 ed.), pp. 260-263. The author of this report used the original Chinese-language version of the report.

[43] Ibid.

[44] The US-China Business Council, "PRC Industry Revitalization Plans (As of may 28, 2009)," p. 1. The 10 critical industries identified in the PRC Industry Revitalization Plans are: auto, steel, equipment manufacturing, textile, shipbuilding, electronics and IT, light industry, petrochemical, logistics, and nonferrous metals.

[45] The US-China Business Council, "USCBC Summary of the PRC Steel Industry Revitalization Plan," p. 1. The author of this report also used the original Chinese-language version of the document, accessible on the official website of The Central People's Government of the People's Republic of China, http://www.gov.cn/zwgk/2009-03/20/content_1264318.htm, as viewed on July 12, 2010.

[46] AMM, "Chinese Premier vows to ax 6M tonnes of steel capacity" (May 7, 2010), p. 9.

[47] AMM, "Beijing orders more steel capacity cuts" (June 4, 2009), p. 9.

[48] AMM, "Chinese mills extend output cuts into Aug." (August 3, 2010).

[49] Steel companies in Beijing, Guangzhou (Guangdong Province), Hangzhou (Zhejiang Province), and Hefei (Anhui Province) will be relocated, according to the Steel Plan.

[50] World Steel Association, "The Chinese steel industry: a monthly update for Worldsteel members" (Issue 45, July 2010).

[51] Financial Times, "China scraps commodity export tax rebates" (June 22, 2010); The Economic Times, "China to scrap export tax rebates on some goods" (June 23, 2010).

[52] Ibid.; World Steel Association, "The Chinese steel industry: a monthly update for Worldsteel members" (Issue 45, July 2010).

[53] World Steel Association, "The Chinese steel industry: a monthly update for Worldsteel members" (Issue 33, July 2009).

[54] AMM, "Chinese finished steel exports down" (August 11, 2010).

[55] Wall Street Journal, "China eases currency peg" (June 20, 2010); For more detailed analysis of China's currency policy and the related economic and trade issues, see CRS Report

RS21625, China's Currency: An Analysis of the Economic Issues, by Wayne M. Morrison and Marc Labonte.
[56] World Steel Association, Steel Statistical Yearbook, pp. 65-66.
[57] AMM, "China ranks as top '09 steel importer" (April 9, 2010).
[58] American Iron and Steel Institute, Annual Statistical Report 2009, Table 20A, p. 53.
[59] Steel Market Intelligence, "ITC imposes duties on Chinese OCTG in final ruling" (December 30, 2009).
[60] Ibid.
[61] Ibid.; USITC News Release 09-108, Inv. Nos. 701-TA-463 (Final) (December 30, 2009); AMM, "ITC votes to impose duties on China OCTG" (January 4, 2010); AMM, "ITC makes final anti-dumping ruling on Chinese OCTG" (May 4, 2010); International Trade Daily, "ITC ruling paves way for AD duties on OCTG from China" (May 4, 2010).
[62] AMM, "ITC votes to impose duties on China OCTG" (January 4, 2010), p. 2.
[63] AMM, "ITC to hear testimony vs. China drill pipe" (January 21, 2010); AMM, "Commerce lunches China drill pipe probe" (January 22, 2010); AMM, "Commerce blasts Chinese drill pipe with high preliminary margins" (August 6, 2010); AMM, "Commerce ruling hits China drill pipe" (August 17, 2010).
[64] AMM, "China pipe hit in Commerce decision" (February 25, 2010); AMM, "Commerce aligns China pipe probes" (March 22, 2010); AMM, "Chinese seamless line pipe slapped with anti-dumping margins" (April 26, 2010).
[65] AMM, "ITC sets hearing in case against Chinese grating" (February 24, 2010); AMM, "Chinese grating firm falsified documents in probe: Commerce" (June 4, 2010); AMM, "ITC votes 6-0 against China grating" (June 25, 2010); AMM, "China gratings safety probe sought" (July 27, 2010). During the investigations, USDOC found that a mandatory Chinese respondent had falsified mill test certificates on the raw materials used to make its grating. The U.S. grating producers became concerned with potential safety issues. They have written to OSHA (the U.S. Occupational Safety and Health Administration) and the U.S. Consumer Product Safety Commission, urging an investigation of steel grating now installed or held in inventory in the United States.
[66] AMM, "Duties set vs. Chinese PC wire strand" (May 19, 2010); AMM, "Chinese PC strands hurt U.S., ITC rules" (June 11, 2010).
[67] AMM, "China wire decking said dumped in U.S." (January 6, 2010); AMM, "China wire decking margins lowered" (June 8, 2010); AMM, "Chinese wire decking makers land ITC victory" (July 2, 2010).
[68] AMM, "U.S. wire decking firms appeal ITC ruling" (August 30, 2010).
[69] AMM, "Chinese again said skirting plate order" (February 22, 2010); AMM, "China plate faces circumvention probe" (April 27, 2010).
[70] AMM, "Chinese boron plate under scrutiny" (July 10, 2009); AMM, "China boron plate traders tried to skirt duty" (August 14, 2009).
[71] On June 23, 2009, the United States and the 27-nation European Union filed the initial complaint at the WTO. Mexico joined the consultations on August 21, 2009.
[72] See USTR November 4, 2009, press release at http://www.ustr.gov/about-us/press-office/press-releases/2009/november/united-states-requests-wto-panel-against-china-ov.
[73] Ibid.; Wall Street Journal, "U.S., Europe file trade complaint against China" (June 24, 2009); Industry Week, "U.S. asks WTO to rule on China's raw materials restrictions" (November 4, 2009); Wall Street Journal, "U.S. requests WTO dispute settlement panel vs. China" (November 4, 2009); Chinese Xinhua News Agency website, "China's restrictions on resource exports consistent with WTO rules: experts," (June 2, 2010),

http://news.xinhuanet.com/ english2010/china/2010-06/02/c_13329535.htm, as viewed on August 19, 2010.
[74] World Trade Organization, Document WT/TPR/G/230, " Trade Policy Review: China" (April 26, 2010), p. 44; Bloomberg.com, "World trade body questions rationale of Chinese raw material export limits" (June 1, 2010).
[75] Wall Street Journal, "Anshan to invest in the U.S." (May 18, 2010); Bloomberg Businessweek, "Anshan agrees to invest in steel project in U.S. for technology" (August 24, 2010); AMM, "Correnti's plans for five U.S. mini-mills under fire" (May 19 , 2010); AMM, "Anshan may land up to 20% stake in SDCO" (June 28, 2010).
[76] AMM, "SMA writes to Commerce, USTR over China investment in SDCO" (May 20, 2010); AMM, "Wall Street's reluctance drives Correnti to China for financing" (May 24, 2010). For more details on bilateral economic relations between China and the United States, see CRS Report RL33536, China-U.S. Trade Issues, by Wayne M. Morrison.
[77] Financial Times, "U.S. lawmakers hit at China steel move" (July 3, 2010); AMM, "Steel Caucus wants probe into SDCO-Anshan deal" (July 2, 2010); AMM, "Steel Caucus voices national security fears" (July 6, 2010).
[78] New York Times, "In seeking Unocal, Chevron ruffles an Asian partner" (July 2, 2005); Bloomberg.com, "CNOOC drops $18.5bln Unocal bid amid U.S. opposition" (August 2, 2005); Business Week, "Why China's Unocal bid ran out of gas" (August 4, 2005).
[79] AMM, "Treasury mum on SDCO-Anshan steel deal" (July 13, 2010); AMM, "Geithner 'aware' of Anshan-SDCO deal" (July 16, 2010); AMM, "Steel Caucus writes to White House on SDCO concerns" (July 30, 2010).
[80] AMM, "SDCO status unclear as Anshan said opting out of investment" (August 19, 2010); AMM, "Anshan says SDCO plan is unchanged" (August 20, 2010); Wall Street Journal, "Anshan's U.S. investment is in doubt" (August 20, 2010); Reuters.com, "China Anshan says still committed to U.S. investment" (August 20, 2010); Wall Street Journal, "Anshan holds to U.S. plan" (August 21, 2010).
[81] AMM, "SDCO, Ansteel tie knot with 14% equity stake" (Sept. 16, 2010); Financial Times, "Anshan defiant amid deal protests" (Sept. 16, 2010).
[82] AMM, "TPCO clears hurdle for Texas pipe mill" (April 16, 2010).
[83] For more detailed analysis of China's currency policy and the related economic and trade issues, see CRS Report RS21625, China's Currency: An Analysis of the Economic Issues, by Wayne M. Morrison and Marc Labonte, and CRS Report RL33536, China-U.S. Trade Issues, by Wayne M. Morrison, pp. 14-16.
[84] AMM, "Trade clampdown effort draws kudos" (August 6, 2010).
[85] Department of Commerce, "Press release: Obama Administration Strengthens Enforcement of U.S. Trade Laws in Support of President's National Export Initiative" (August 26, 2010); AMM, "Commerce secretary Locke lays out trade law proposal" (August 27, 2010).
[86] AMM, "Steel lauds trade law proposal, but wants currency addressed" (August 26, 2010).
[87] News release on USW website, "USW files trade case to preserve clean, green manufacturing jobs in America," http://www.usw.org/media_center/releases_advisories?id=0327, as viewed on September 9, 2010; New York Times, "Steelworkers accuse China of violating trade rules" (September 9, 2010).
[88] http://www.osec.doc.gov/ogc/occic/301.html, as viewed on September 9, 2010: "Section 301 of the Trade Act of 1974 is the principal statutory authority under which the U.S. may impose trade sanctions against foreign countries that maintains acts, policies and practices that violate, or deny U.S. right s or benefits under, trade agreements, or are unjustifiable, unreasonable or discriminatory and burden or restrict U.S. commerce."

In: U.S. Manufacturing Dogfights
Editors: Jeffrey A. Ball

ISBN: 978-1-62100-672-5
© 2012 Nova Science Publishers, Inc

Chapter 2

CHALLENGE TO THE BOEING-AIRBUS DUOPOLY IN CIVIL AIRCRAFT: ISSUES FOR COMPETITIVENESS[*]

Glennon J. Harrison

SUMMARY

The importance of a successful aerospace industry to the United States economy has been repeatedly acknowledged by President Obama and members of his Cabinet, many Members of Congress, and by all concerned with the competitive fortunes of the U.S. aircraft manufacturing industry. The U.S. aerospace industry is highly competitive and global in scope. U.S. firms manufacture a wide range of products for civil and defense purposes and, in 2010, the value of aerospace industry shipments was estimated at $171 billion, of which civil aircraft and aircraft parts accounted for over half of all U.S. aerospace shipments. In 2010, the U.S. aerospace industry exported nearly $78 billion in products, of which $67 billion (or 86% of total exports) were civil aircraft, engines, equipment, and parts. The U.S. trade surplus (net exports) in aerospace products in 2010 was $43.6 billion – higher than for any other manufacturing industry. Aerospace employment totaled 477,000 workers, of which 228,400 were engaged in the manufacture of aircraft, 76,400 in the manufacture of engines and engine

---

[*] This is an edited, reformatted and augmented version of a Congressional Research Service publication, CRS Report for Congress R41925, from www.crs.gov, dated July 25, 2011.

parts, and 97,600 in the manufacture of other parts and equipment. According to the International Trade Administration, "more jobs in the United States were supported by exports of U.S. aerospace products than of any other manufacturing or service industry."

Boeing is the only U.S. manufacturer of large civil aircraft. Civil aircraft engines are manufactured by General Electric (GE), in partnership with Safran (of France), and by Pratt & Whitney. Numerous firms manufacture sections and parts of the airframe, as well as original equipment for both domestic and foreign airframe manufacturers. The civil and military aerospace sectors are complementary in that many firms manufacture products for both. Although the products tend to be dissimilar, workforce skills are transferable, so a decline in military aerospace budgets or private sector spending on civil aircraft have significant economic and competitive effects for the United States.

A major issue for policymakers is whether the United States can sustain its preeminent position in aerospace, given the intentions of numerous foreign manufacturers to enter the small commercial jet aircraft segment by 2016. That segment accounts for nearly half of all commercial aircraft revenues and for more than 60% of commercial aircraft deliveries. It is also the gateway to building larger commercial aircraft. Boeing and Airbus are the sole rivals across all segments of large commercial aircraft manufacturing, but during the next decade both will confront a potentially serious challenge in one of the most important segments of their business, small commercial jets (which are also referred to as narrow-body or single-aisle aircraft). The CEOs of Boeing and Airbus have both agreed that their duopoly over small commercial jets is nearly at an end.

Boeing and Airbus will face competition from government-owned and subsidized firms in Russia and China, as well as companies in Canada, Brazil, and Japan. Several factors will determine the outcome of the coming competition in small commercial jets, including the openness of markets to foreign commercial aircraft and aircraft engines and parts; whether state-owned aircraft manufacturers continue to receive substantial government subsidies; whether the challengers to Boeing and Airbus achieve their goal of building innovative, efficient aircraft that establish excellent safety and service records; whether airlines will buy aircraft from companies that have no track record; and the effect of collaborative partnerships with other aircraft manufacturers and suppliers as a strategy for success. Boeing and Airbus are engaged in a struggle to be the world's preeminent manufacturer of civil aircraft and both have a depth of resources unmatched elsewhere. The competitive stakes for both companies will be very high during the next decade.

CHALLENGE TO THE BOEING-AIRBUS DUOPOLY IN CIVIL AIRCRAFT: ISSUES FOR COMPETITIVENESS

The importance of a successful aerospace industry to the United States economy has been repeatedly acknowledged by President Obama and members of his Cabinet, many Members of Congress, and by all concerned with the competitive fortunes of the U.S. aircraft manufacturing industry. The U.S. aerospace industry is highly competitive and global in scope. Numerous U.S. firms manufacture a wide range of products for civil and defense purposes. In 2010, the value of aerospace industry shipments was estimated at $171 billion, of which civil aircraft and aircraft parts accounted for approximately half ($85 billion) of all U.S. aerospace shipments.[1]

In 2010, the U.S. aerospace industry exported nearly $78 billion in products, of which $67 billion (or 86% of total exports) were civil aircraft, engines, equipment, and parts.[2] The only U.S. manufacturer of large civil aircraft is Boeing. Civil aircraft engines are manufactured by General Electric (GE) in partnership with Safran (of France) and by Pratt & Whitney. Numerous firms manufacture sections and parts of the airframe, as well as original equipment for both domestic and foreign airframe manufacturers. The U.S. trade surplus (net exports) in aerospace products in 2010 was $43.6 billion – higher than for any other manufacturing industry.[3] In 2010, the aerospace sector employed 477,000 workers, of which 228,400 were engaged in the manufacture of aircraft, 76,400 in the manufacture of engines and engine parts, and 97,600 in the manufacture of other parts and equipment. According to the International Trade Administration (ITA), "more jobs in the United States were supported by exports of U.S. aerospace products than of any other manufacturing or service industry."[4] A major issue for policymakers is whether the United States can sustain its preeminent position in aerospace, given the intentions of numerous foreign manufacturers to enter the small commercial jet aircraft segment by 2016.[5] That segment accounts for nearly half of commercial aircraft revenues and for more than 60% of commercial aircraft deliveries.

Some industry participants and analysts have recently suggested that the two dominant manufacturers of large civil aircraft, Boeing and Airbus, now face a new and significant group of competitors that are ready to challenge the incumbents for a potentially significant share of the market for small commercial jets. Currently that market is almost wholly owned by the Boeing

737 and Airbus A320 families of jets. In Boeing's *2010 Annual Report*, W. James McNerny, Jr., chairman, president, and CEO of Boeing, writes:

> At Boeing Commercial Airplanes, we must prepare now for increasing global competition. Aircraft manufacturers in several countries are poised to challenge us for a share of the market where we have been competing solely against EADS/Airbus. These emerging competitors see the same massive economic opportunity in commercial airplanes and related services that we do over the next 20 to 30 years.[6]

On June 20, 2011, the opening day of the 2011 Paris Air Show, the president of Boeing Commercial Airplanes, Jim Albaugh, announced "the days of the duopoly with Airbus are over."[7] Albaugh was referring to long-standing dominance that Boeing and Airbus have held over the commercial jet aircraft business and, in particular, to the 90-220 seat aircraft segment that has seemingly come into play with the entry of competitors from Brazil, Canada, China, Russia, and Japan.

Tom Enders, the chief executive officer of Airbus, agreed in part, saying "the duopoly is over in the 100 to 150 seat aircraft segment because that is where the new entrants ... want to be – so that doesn't mean the duopoly is over in the entire range of products."[8] Enders also mentioned that he doubted that there was room for six competitors and that "we think sooner or later there will be some consolidation."[9] If the small commercial jet segment is about to enter a new competitive phase, there is no evidence that the dominance of Airbus and Boeing over large (or wide-body) aircraft or very large (or super-jumbo) aircraft will face a similar challenge anytime soon.

The small commercial jet segment represents a significant share of U.S. aerospace manufacturing sector output (see text box above for a discussion of aircraft types). In 2010, Boeing delivered 462 aircraft, of which 376 (81%) were Boeing 737s. Boeing also reported that it booked 486 net 737 orders in 2010, and had a firm order book of 2,186 737s as of December 31, 2010. Boeing's rival, Airbus, delivered 510 aircraft, of which 401 (79%) were A320s.[10] Airbus booked 416 net orders for the A320 Family and had an order backlog of 2,418 A320 airplanes.[11]

Boeing and Airbus will likely face intense and determined competitors that see an opportunity to manufacture large civil aircraft in the 90–220 seat range. However, with the exception of Embraer's 190 and 195 E-Jets, none of the new competitors have yet to build any of the planes that they claim will be superior to Boeing and Airbus products.[12] Both Boeing and Airbus recognize the possibility that one or more aircraft manufacturers may succeed in building planes that will compete with the Boeing 737 and the Airbus A320 families. Boeing's Jim McNerny has to do little more than look at Airbus – a company formed in 1970 by three European governments to ensure that a previously fragmented European aerospace industry would survive – to recognize that additional competitors have the potential to fundamentally change the global aircraft manufacturing industry. But history has not been kind to a market crowded with suppliers of commercial jet aircraft.

Large Commercial Aircraft Types: Definitions

Commercial aircraft are defined in terms of market segments, but definitions are fluid and various segments overlap each other. In its 2010 forecast, Boeing defines aircraft as single-aisle passenger airplanes, twin-aisle passenger airplanes, and freighter airplanes (this report is primarily concerned with commercial passenger aircraft and will not discuss freighter aircraft in detail). Boeing further subdivides single-aisle and twin-aisle passenger planes into subcategories. Single aisle aircraft comprise: regional jets (RJs) and narrow-body aircraft (in two classes: 90-175 seat airplanes and >175 seat airplanes). Twin-aisle airplanes (frequently referred to as "wide-bodies" and "large" passenger aircraft) are categorized by Boeing as small (180-340 seats), medium (260-450 seats), and large (>400 seats). Large twin-aisle passenger airplanes (e.g. the Boeing 747 and Airbus A380) are also referred to as very large aircraft (VLA). The most recent models of the Boeing 737 and Airbus A320 aircraft (the 737-900ER and the A321) can seat up to 215 and 220 passengers, respectively. Because the 737-900ER and the A321 do not differ significantly from other models in those aircraft families (except for capacity), this report will treat all members of the 737 and A320 families as single-aisle, narrow-body airplanes. For example, the width and height of the 737 fuselage remained the same from its first flight in 1967 through the most recent model, the 737-900ER, which was first delivered in 2007.

Boeing and Airbus are the dominant producers of narrow-body commercial transport aircraft 90- 220 seats). Two other aircraft manufacturers, Bombardier and Embraer, are the dominant producers of regional jets (RJs, which are defined as having fewer than 90 seats) and also manufacture narrow-body aircraft.[13] The entry of new competitors into both the RJ and narrow-body markets could result in a much higher level of competition for both the dominant RJ manufacturers (Bombardier and Embraer) and the dominant narrow-body manufacturers (Airbus and Boeing).

All of the new entrants are almost certain to face a number of hurdles that will determine whether they succeed, go back to the drawing board, or exit large commercial aircraft manufacturing.

Chinese, Russian, and Japanese manufacturers have not previously built *commercially competitive* large civil aircraft, and Canada's Bombardier and Brazil's Embraer have primarily manufactured regional jets, albeit with considerable success. The complexities that aircraft integrators, such as Boeing and Airbus, have faced with various aircraft development programs (including recent programs such as the Airbus A380 and A350 and the Boeing 787) would be sufficient to sink all but the strongest aerospace companies. However, because some of the new entrants into the large civil aircraft sector are state-owned and -controlled companies (i.e., Russia's United Aircraft Corporation and China's Commercial Aircraft Corporation of China) that are funded by the government, commercial considerations may be less important during the development phase of the Russian and Chinese commercial aerospace projects.

GROWING DEMAND FOR NARROW-BODY AIRCRAFT: A MARKET SIGNAL TO NEW ENTRANTS?

One of the major market drivers for new narrow-body and RJ aircraft is projected high demand for efficient narrow-body aircraft in markets that are expected to grow rapidly during the next 20 years, especially in Asia and Latin America. The other major driver is the anticipated retirement of many of the airplanes in the current narrow-body fleet. Expected high demand for aircraft has attracted additional manufacturers, especially those that have the technical capacity to build such planes or those who possess a rapidly growing market for these, such as China and potentially India.

Some of the new entrants have programs to build RJs that seat 70-90 passengers, but they could reasonably be expected to build larger aircraft in the not too distant future. Others are developing narrow-body aircraft that their manufacturers expect will compete head-to-head with the Boeing 737 and Airbus A320 families of narrow-body jets. The manufacturers of the new aircraft claim their planes will deliver substantially greater fuel efficiency than current versions of the 737 or A320 families, although it remains to be seen if the new planes will actually do so.[14]

Table 1. In Production, Launched, and Out-of-Production Regional Jets and Single-aisle Narrow-Body Aircraft

Regional Jets (34-89 seats)	Narrow-body, Single Aisle Jets (90-220 seats)
Antonov An-148[a]	Boeing 707, 717, 727, 757[b]
AVIC ARJ-700	Boeing 737-100 through 500
Avro RJ70, 85	**Boeing 737-600/700/800/900ER**
BAe 146-100	**Airbus A318, A319, A320, A321**
Bombardier CRJ	Boeing-MDC DC-9, MD-80, -90
Dornier 328JET	**AVIC ARJ-900**
Embraer 170, 175	BAe 146-300, Avro RJ100
Embraer ERJ-135/140/145	**Bombardier CRJ-1000**
Fokker 70, F28	**Bombardier CS100, CS300**
Mitsubishi MRJ	**COMAC C919**
Sukhoi Superjet 100	**Embraer 190, 195**
Yakovlev Yak-40	Fokker 100
	Ilyushin IL-62
	Tupelov TU-154
	Tupelov TU-204, TU-214
	Yakovlev Yak-42

Source: Boeing, Current Market Outlook 2011-2030.
Notes: This table does not follow the Boeing classification scheme, which divides non-RJ, single-aisle planes into two categories ("90-175 seats" and "More than 175 seats"). This table combines all single-aisle, narrow-body jets into one column because the trend has been for narrow-body jets, including the Boeing 737 and Airbus A320 families, to grow larger.
[a] Bolded text indicates an airplane that is in production or launched (i.e., in development). Unbolded text indicates airplanes that are no longer in production.
[b] The Boeing 757 is a large single-aisle narrow-body jet that seats from 200 passengers (in a two-class configuration to 289 passengers in a single-class configuration.) The 757 has not been produced since 2004.

Several of the entrants to the narrow-body and RJ markets are well established aircraft manufacturers or are producers of major sections of airframes for others. The established firms include Bombardier (Canada), Embraer (Brazil), and Mitsubishi Heavy Industries (MHI)(Japan). Others, such as United Aircraft Corporation (UAC)(Russia) and Commercial Aircraft Corporation of China (COMAC)(China), are new firms that reflect a reorganization of existing state-owned aerospace (defense and commercial) manufacturing resources by Russia and China. Their intent is to create industries that are viable international competitors. Both UAC and COMAC will produce RJs and narrow-body aircraft in cooperative partnerships with Western suppliers (see Table 1).

With the entry of additional competitors, the major producers of narrow-body airplanes (Boeing/Airbus) and RJs (Bombardier/Embraer) will potentially face disruptive competition. All of the newcomers will have to build market share quickly if their airplanes are to achieve viability. Bombardier and COMAC have signed a partnership agreement and are developing complementary, but non-overlapping, narrow-body airplanes that will seat 100-149 passengers (Bombardier) and 156-190 passengers (COMAC).[15] This partnership may pose the most serious challenge to the Boeing/Airbus narrow-body franchise if COMAC and Bombardier are able to gain a significant share of the fast-growing Chinese market – a market that both Boeing and Airbus intend to contest. Embraer, which had considered and rejected stretching its 190/195 E-jet (98-122 seats), may also decide to build a larger narrow-body airplane, especially if China, Russia, and Japan move into Embraer's core RJ market.[16] Embraer is considering the development of a new larger airplane, but has not yet announced whether it will proceed, a decision that may ultimately depend on Boeing's plans and schedule for developing a replacement aircraft for the 737.[17]

Boeing and Airbus are, at present, the premier manufacturers of large civil aircraft of all sizes, but the importance of narrow-body aircraft to both companies cannot be overstated. According to Boeing's forecast for 2011-2030, narrow-body jets are expected to account for about 60% of all sales and about 47% of all revenues during the period. Although the two companies have, in recent years, sold roughly equivalent numbers of narrow-body planes, the projected demand for 23,330 narrow-body airplanes through 2030 suggests that the market may be theirs to lose if they do not keep ahead of the competition or if they are not capable of producing enough airplanes to meet their customers' demands.[18]

Airbus has announced that it will upgrade the A320 family by 2015, offering two new models of high efficiency engines. Airbus has announced that it does not intend to develop a replacement for the A320 until the mid-2020s. On July 20, 2011, Boeing followed Airbus' lead and announced that it would re-engine the 737 rather than replace it with a new small aircraft by 2020. Neither company appears to take competition (with each other or with newcomers) for granted, but both companies appear to believe the risks that the newcomers are willing to assume will be greater than those that should taken by market leaders with strong reputations for building commercial aircraft. Boeing and Airbus, with complete access to the latest aerospace technologies, may believe that they can learn from the experience of the newcomers without compromising safety, their overall competitiveness, or their ability to deliver a plane within a time-frame necessary to remain competitive.

AIRCRAFT DEVELOPMENT: A HIGH STAKES VENTURE

The decision to develop (or "launch") a new airplane exposes commercial aircraft builders, jet engine manufacturers, and a host of other suppliers to very high levels of risk. Throughout the twentieth century, most firms made losing bets on aircraft and exited the commercial market entirely.

Various types of risk are associated with aircraft development, including a manufacturer's ability to access capital markets to bring a plane to market; to deliver a plane that meets the performance requirements that were promised to launch customers; to deliver the plane in a timely manner; to attract sufficient customer demand to recover launch costs and earn a profit; and to anticipate the response of competitors.

Investment Risk

Large capital investments are required to bring a new plane to market. For publicly traded, shareholder-owned (as opposed to state-owned) corporations that manufacture commercial aircraft, the inability to raise launch capital would be sufficient to doom most projects. For commercial aircraft manufacturers, the overall risks associated with the launch of a new airplane is high enough that the term "betting the company" is frequently used to describe it. According to the U.S. International Trade Commission (USITC), "the development costs incurred by Boeing in 1966 for its 747 program are estimated to have been $1.2 billion – more than triple Boeing's total capitalization at that time."[19] In other words, Boeing's level of risk was sufficiently high that failure could have brought the company down. Airlines and aircraft leasing corporations also bear similar risks: the purchase of a new airplane requires an airline to either borrow to finance the new airplanes or, as many airlines do, lease the new aircraft from one of the many companies that offer planes for lease. However, in the event that a particular aircraft does not generate enough sales to justify its place in the market, a launch customer (whether it be an airline or an aircraft leasing company) does not want to be the largest or only operator/owner of an airplane that is deemed a commercial failure.

Fleet Complexity

For airlines, who are the main customers of large civil aircraft manufacturers, fleet complexity provides flexibility but increases costs because of the need to support additional and different parts inventories and multiple training programs for aircraft crews and maintenance personnel. Fleet complexity emerges by design or by merger. It has been common for airlines to map out (or expand) a network and then acquire aircraft that best fit the needs of that network, or to outsource parts of the network to regional carriers that use RJs to feed the major airlines at their hubs. This was the strategy favored by legacy carriers (most of the airlines that predate airline deregulation in 1978). Bankruptcies and numerous airline mergers have also contributed significantly to fleet complexity, as large numbers of very different aircraft types were integrated into the merged enterprise. Fleet complexity is frequently necessary to support a varying mix of short- and medium-haul domestic and long-haul international operations.

The major weakness of fleet complexity is the impact of changing business conditions on airlines. Rapidly fluctuating fuel costs or a sharp drop in the number of passengers (due, for instance, to a recession or economic downturn) have potentially greater negative effects on airlines that purchased aircraft to fit a network than on airlines that built a network on the basis of a specific type of aircraft. After airline deregulation, many airlines sought to compete for the same high density routes. This competition frequently created overcapacity, and resulted in low passenger yields and low fares on high density routes – a business model that practically guaranteed poor financial results. Deregulation also resulted in the abandonment by airlines of many routes that generated too few passengers to be profitable – leaving some communities with limited service and few direct flights other than to the nearest hub or with no service at all. Many of the flights to "thin" markets use smaller turboprops or RJs flown by regional carriers under contract to legacy carriers.

In contrast, numerous low-cost carriers constructed networks based on a fleet of only one or two types of aircraft, including Southwest (737); AirTran (717, 737),[20] JetBlue (Airbus A320, Embraer 190), and Ryan Air (737) of

Ireland, among many others. This strategy has proved effective for growth and has allowed airlines like Southwest to move into territories that were once controlled by large legacy carriers.

Fleet complexity has direct and indirect effects on aircraft manufacturers. Aircraft manufacturers have found it easier to compete against one another for an airline's business if the airline owns various models of airplanes made by multiple aircraft manufacturers. Aircraft manufacturers typically work closely with launch customers to create an airplane that meets customer requirements. This has frequently led to bidding wars among major aircraft makers, which sometimes offer airplanes to launch customers at unrealistically low prices, which then requires the manufacturer to sell many more planes to reach a breakeven point.[21]

Conversely, an airline that builds its network around one manufacturer/one type of aircraft creates a network effect that results in "lock-in." A low-cost carrier with a network based on one aircraft model has little incentive to purchase a comparable airplane from another manufacturer, even if the upfront price of the alternative airliner is attractive. In the case of Southwest Airlines, this strategy works well for Boeing, but effectively locks-out other competitors as long as they do not produce a competing product that is so recognizably superior to the Boeing 737 that Southwest has little choice but to switch. On the other hand, the current generation of 737s appears to be moving toward the end of its product life cycle in terms of the technological improvements and efficiency gains that can be made to it.

For a number of months, Boeing engaged in a lively debate with its customers and itself about building a newer, more technologically advanced plane to replace the 737 by the end of the current decade. Southwest, Boeing's largest customer, has said that the replacement for the 737 is needed sooner rather than later. Against this customer pressure to replace the 737, the immediate success of the A320neo (new engine option) increased pressure on Boeing to put new, more efficient engines onto the 737, thus prolonging the life of one of the best known planes flying today. However, American Airlines, an all-Boeing customer, announced on July 20, 2011 a massive order for 430 narrow-body jets. In splitting its order between the A320 and 737, American announced that given its need to acquire the planes rapidly, no one company could deliver the all of the planes quickly enough.

For those manufacturers that do not currently control a significant share of the 90-200 seat aircraft market, whether Canadian, Brazilian, Chinese, Russian, or Japanese, the larger challenge will be to produce and sell a commercial product that is superior to the planes currently on offer by Airbus and Boeing.[22] The prospect that Airbus and Boeing may deliver more efficient planes in a timeframe that approximates the challengers' schedules further complicates their ability to claim existing market share from Boeing and Airbus.

The difficulties, however, are more complex than building a more efficient airplane. Jet aircraft require a significant support network that is capable of supplying parts and assistance on a 24/7 basis with next-day delivery anywhere those planes fly. A plane that cannot fly because a part is not available cannot earn revenue, and airlines cannot afford to have a $50–$250 million piece of equipment sitting on the tarmac waiting on a part for very long. Bombardier and Embraer have both demonstrated that they can support the airlines that operate their aircraft. Russian aircraft manufacturers have traditionally had a poor reputation for service and parts supply. Russian and Chinese aircraft companies have announced that support services will be accomplished via joint ventures with European or North American partners. A proposed link between Bombardier and COMAC may help the Chinese manufacturer sell planes in some foreign markets.

Reputational Risk, Uncertainty, and Inefficiency

Reputational risk could be a significant problem for some manufacturers. This type of risk stems from many sources, but primarily affects the willingness of airlines and airline leasing companies to make large financial commitments to aircraft manufacturers that have not previously achieved success in competitive markets or who are new to the aircraft market segment they are entering. It seems highly unlikely that a major U.S. or European airline would commit to purchase a large number of expensive aircraft built by companies that have a limited track record and a poor reputation for after-sales support and quick parts delivery. Even if the airplanes are certificated in Europe or the United States, passenger airlines that purchase Russian-built airplanes could alienate their customers. From a competitive perspective, it will probably take years of solid service (including maintenance and parts support), possibly in the fleet of a reputable European air cargo operator, to convince passenger airlines and their customers that the airplane can deliver a level of service equivalent to that of Boeing and Airbus aircraft.

One reason for concern is that the major aircraft manufacturers in the Soviet Union (Ilyushin, Sukhoi, Antonov, and Yakovlev) were protected from competition and market forces for decades prior to the collapse of the Soviet

Union. With the breakup of the Soviet Union, none of the Russian companies could produce a commercial airplane that was competitive against products by Boeing or Airbus. By 2005, the entire Russian aircraft manufacturing industry was producing an average of 10 commercial aircraft a year.[23] A widely held view is that the major problem with Russian commercial aircraft was poor after-sales support and poor maintenance by the airlines that operated the airplanes.[24] The collapse of the Russian aircraft industry led to its reorganization by the Russian government in 2006. The new umbrella company, United Aircraft Corporation (UAC), is more than 92% owned by the Russian Federation and the Russian Development Bank (*Vnesheconombank*).[25] With government support, Sukhoi has launched the SuperJet 100, a regional jet, and Irkut is developing the MS-21, a narrow-body (150-210 seat) airplane that will compete directly with Airbus A320 and Boeing 737 aircraft.

The outlook for the Russian civil air transport sector, however, is problematic. In a 2008 study, the U.S. Commerce Department, citing the Russian Transport Ministry, reported that "by 2005, of the 2,528 total civil aircraft currently in service, more than one-half had passed their legal operational limits and needed replacing...[and]...industry experts forecast that Russian airlines would need at least 620...aircraft in the next 20 years."[26] Boeing's 2010 forecast for the Commonwealth of Independent States (C.I.S.), a group comprising Russia and eight former Soviet republics, projects that the region will acquire 960 new commercial airplanes between 2010 and 2029, with a market value of $90 billion (in 2009 dollars). The new aircraft will have an average value of $90 million each (in 2009 dollars). The number of commercial airplanes in the C.I.S. in 2009 was 1,150 and is projected to rise to 1,300 in 2029 – an annual rate of 0.6%. Most of the new deliveries will replace older equipment.[27] With limited future demand for new commercial airplanes in Russia and the rest of the C.I.S., Russian manufacturers will have to compete against both new and used Boeing and Airbus airplanes in non-C.I.S. markets where high demand is anticipated or where demand for replacement aircraft is high.

In contrast to Russia and the other C.I.S. countries, the outlook for China is highly positive. Boeing projects that Chinese demand for new aircraft between 2009 and 2029 will be 4,330 new airplanes, with a market value of $480 billion (in 2009 dollars), with an average airplane value of $110 million (in 2009 dollars). Of new deliveries, 71% are projected to be narrow-body airplanes and only 6% are expected to be regional jets.

To overcome the reputation issue, both Russian-owned UAC and Chinese-owned COMAC have sought well established international joint venture partners that will be involved in the design, manufacture, marketing, and maintenance of commercial aircraft manufactured by those state-owned companies. Their expectation is that such partnerships will increase credibility and reduce the risk to airlines that purchase or lease such planes – especially if the partnerships help those companies establish a reputation for product safety, performance, quality, comfort, and price competitiveness. Such partnerships may benefit the various partners in the short-run, but as the new aircraft firms gain confidence and market share, both Russian and Chinese companies are likely to seek higher levels of national (or indigenous) competency and competitiveness across the range of advanced technologies (e.g., engines, wing, and avionics and other systems) and after-sale support.

COMAC, the state-owned Chinese commercial aircraft company, has set out a number of basic principles for the development of a narrow-body aircraft that includes bringing into "full play the political superiority of the socialist system," competitiveness with Western products, commercial independence, and "independent intellectual property rights." These raise the possibility of a captive domestic market in which Chinese airlines will buy COMAC airplanes – even if they prove to be inferior to competing products (see text box below).[28] The Chinese commercial aircraft industry is currently at a stage of developing domestic capabilities that require complex cooperative partnerships with foreign (chiefly European and American) suppliers. But COMAC's principles suggest an agenda that envisions a national policy of economic independence for its aircraft industry and possibly its aircraft market – a more autarkic vision that appears to differ from those of companies that are pursuing market opportunities within a free trade context in China and elsewhere.

In markets where the state owns or controls both the aircraft manufacturing industry and airlines (China, in particular), governments can apply pressure to ensure that airlines purchase domestically produced aircraft. In combination with industrial policies that could potentially hinder market access by foreign aircraft manufacturers, a protected market for aircraft sales could easily guarantee sufficient local demand to allow a domestic producer to achieve scale economies. Of course, the Chinese market is sufficiently large that it should be capable of supporting domestic production and imports. The question is whether China will protect the market for its own narrow-body and regional jet aircraft while continuing to purchase aircraft that it cannot yet produce (i.e. wide-body medium and large aircraft). Whether Airbus or Boeing could challenge such an approach without fear of retaliation (loss of sales of large airliners to large state-owned airlines) remains to be seen.

> **COMAC: Basic Principles of Developing the C919**
>
> - Chinese Characteristics. We should set our footing on the practical situations in China, leverage on the whole nation's strengths and wisd[o]m, and bring into full play the political superiority of the socialist system which is capable of concentrating all of its resources in achieving great things.
> - Cutting-edge Technology. We must consider user needs in the beginning during design and make sure the trunk liners that we are going to develop and manufacture will be competitive with other products in the same class.
> - Strategic cooperation. We will commit to national and international cooperation based on the "airframersuppliers" model to share risks and benefits, and build a system of both national and international suppliers for trunk liner, and eventually establish relatively complete service and industrial chains in the commercial airplane business.
> - Innovative System and Mechanism. We should establish the notion and use of systematic engineering to promote innovations in systems and mechanisms, as well as in management.
> - Independent Intellectual Property Rights. In order to meet the demand of the domestic aviation market, we should comply with the safety, economy, comfort and environmental regulations of the aviation authorities and acqui[r]e ownership of our independent intellectual property rights.
>
> Note: Text is verbatim from the Commercial Aircraft Corporation of China website.
> Source: Commercial Aircraft Corporation of China (COMAC) website: http://english.comac.cc/products/ca/pi/index.shtml

THE CHANGING ECONOMICS OF SMALL COMMERCIAL JETS

The Boeing 737 and Airbus A320 families of airplanes (see Figure 1 for an illustration of the various models in the Airbus A320 family) overwhelmingly define the narrow-body, single-aisle market.[29] Sales of 737s and A320s provide the bulk of orders and earnings for both Boeing Commercial Airplanes (BCA), based in Renton, WA, and Airbus SAS, based in Toulouse, France.[30] These companies have been the sole competitors for the large commercial aircraft market since Boeing and McDonnell Douglas merged in 1997.[31] Boeing is the sole U.S. producer of large commercial aircraft. Unlike many other manufacturers of aircraft, Boeing and Airbus are the only companies that produce a complete range of mainline commercial aircraft (small narrow-body to very large aircraft). The Boeing Company and EADS, Airbus' parent company, are also major international defense aerospace contractors. The Brazilian aerospace company, Embraer, produces the 190 and 195 E-Jets, which competes with smaller narrow-body planes by Airbus (the A318) and Boeing (the 737-600 series).[32]

Source: Airbus.

Figure 1. The Airbus A320 Family of Jet Aircraft; A318, A319, A320, and A321.

Large civil aircraft are typically used for 25 years or more before being sold to cargo fleets, nonscheduled carriers, or to foreign airlines that lack the resources to buy newer equipment. Some narrow-body passenger aircraft, including the DC-9, have flown in U.S. airline fleets for up to 40 years. The first Boeing 737s (the 100 and 200 series) were delivered in December 1967 – or 43 years ago.[33] Because of the longevity of commercial aircraft, manufacturer's must consider the entire life-cycle of the plane and the likelihood that there will continue to be a market for the jet for more than enough years to cover the development costs of the plane.

Airlines use aircraft intensively for many years and incur various operating costs that play a critical role in measuring aircraft performance. Costs include salaries, wages, and benefits; fuel and oil; maintenance materials and repairs; landing fees and other rentals; depreciation and amortization; aircraft rentals; and other expenses. According to Southwest Airlines' most recent annual report, "except for changes in the price of fuel, changes in operating expenses for airlines are largely driven by changes in capacity, or [available seat miles] ASMs."[34]

The demand for commercial aircraft changed in significant ways during the last decade in response to a number of exogenous events, including 9/11 and the shock experienced by the aerospace industry as a whole; the deep recession of 2008-2009; and fuel costs that have generally been rising since 2004. Since 2008, the volatility of fuel prices have caused significant problems for the airline industry (see Figure 2). During a five-month period in 2008, airlines were buffeted by crude oil spot prices that peaked at $147/barrel (bbl.) before falling below $35/bbl. Again in April 2011, the refiner acquisition cost of a barrel of crude oil rose to approximately $112, or nearly $28 higher per barrel than the year before.[35] The 2008 and 2011 spikes in fuel costs, associated with oil prices greater than $100 per barrel, is part of what spurred airlines to increase load factors by reducing the number of available seats miles (i.e., retiring or parking aircraft);[36] reduce excess network capacity by reducing the number of scheduled flights and discontinuing service to some cities; eliminate formerly profitable 50-seat regional jets from many routes; increase ticket prices and impose "ancillary fees" for baggage and numerous other services;[37] and retire many older aircraft and demand more fuel-efficient replacements.

Airlines have constrained capacity by grounding many older planes and reducing the number of flights from 11.6 million per year in 2005 to 10.1 million per year in 2010. For the period between 1978, the year airlines were deregulated, and 2002, system-wide (domestic and international) load factors for all U.S. airlines averaged 64.5%. Between 2003 and 2010, load factors rose dramatically from 73.5% to 82.1% – the highest levels ever achieved. Together with the consolidation that has occurred within the airline industry and the numerous fees that airlines are using to boost revenues, the outlook for the industry has improved.

Although maintenance, repair, and overhaul (MRO) spending generally amounts to less than 10% of total annual operating expenses, long lasting assets, such as airframes and engines, require ongoing maintenance and repairs, as well as overhauls as planes age. Over the course of an aircraft's lifespan, engines account for 46% of maintenance, repair, and overhaul (MRO) spending, while airframes account for the rest. Total global MRO spending was $42.6 billion in 2010.[38]

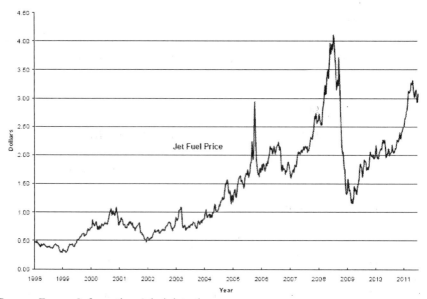

Source: Energy Information Administration.

Figure 2. Price of Jet Fuel (January 1998 – July 8, 2011); Weekly U.S. Gulf Coast Kerosene-Type Jet Fuel Spot Price FOB (Dollars per Gallon).

Many older airliners are being retired, including the Boeing 737-300/400/500 series (also called the "737 Classic" series) that seats 122-159 passengers depending on the specific model and seating configuration), the MD-80/90 series, the DC-9, and older model Airbus A320s.[39] At the same time, the economics of regional jets have also changed. With high fuel prices, once profitable 50-seat RJs have become money-losers and airlines have shifted to larger aircraft.[40]

Figure 3 provides a chart that shows the average stage length (left axis of chart) of narrow-body mainline jets and wide-body jets and operating cost per ASM (CASM)(right axis of chart).[41] In Figure 3, the single-aisle narrow-body planes with the shortest average stage length usually have higher operating costs per available seat mile (CASM). The age of the plane also plays a role.

The DC-9s, some of the oldest planes, have the highest cost per available seat mile, followed by the "737 Classic" series.[42]

AIRCRAFT INVESTMENTS AND FORECASTING

The Federal Aviation Administration (FAA) and major aircraft companies produce an annual 20- year forecast for the aviation industry and markets. These forecasts consider numerous factors that weigh on the market for commercial aircraft, including carrier schedules, passenger load factors, average aircraft size, the average length of flights (or stages, which involve one take-off and one landing), airspace and airport capacities, fuel costs, and different rates of growth of various regions of the world economy, among many other variables. The various segments of the industry interact in a complex manner and there are many unknowns that can quickly undercut the accuracy of any forecast. Nevertheless, forecasts guide planners as they make very large investment decisions about the production and purchase of aircraft, infrastructure development, air traffic control modernization, and regulation. The forecasts provide guidance both to the private sector and to policymakers.

The range of narrow-body models produced by both Boeing and Airbus are designed to complement almost any fleet and, in some cases, comprise the entire fleet (e.g., Southwest: 737s; Virgin America: A319s and A320s; Ryanair: 737s). During the 2000-2010 period, more than 11,000 narrow-body units were delivered or on backlog. Because demand for narrow-body airplanes was so strong, production at Boeing and Airbus did not slump during the 2008-2009 recession.[43] From 2000 through 2010, Boeing 737 orders averaged 395 per year. In 2010, Boeing 737 deliveries numbered a record 376 planes. According to Boeing, "The 737 program currently produces 31.5 airplanes per month and expects to go to 35 per month in early 2012, 38 per month in second quarter 2013 and then to 42 per month in the first half of 2014."[44] With Boeing 737 backorders of 2,101 airplanes as of May 31, 2011, it would take Boeing nearly 5.6 years (until the end of 2016) to deliver the current backlog of orders at current rates. At the end of May 2011, Airbus had backorders of 2,420 of the A320 family of aircraft and had also announced that it would gradually increase production of the A320 to 42 per month.[45] The most recent order from American Airlines and an anticipated order from Delta Air Lines may raise production levels at both companies by as much as 20 additional planes a month.

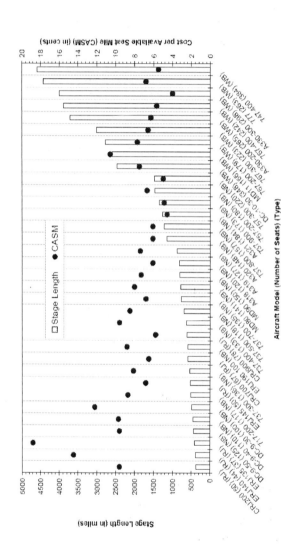

Figure 3.

Source: This graph was prepared by CRS and is based on data published in *Aviation Week Intelligence Network* as presented in various spreadsheets published by *Aviation Daily* in February and March 2011. Data are based on Federal Aviation Administration Form 41 data analyzed by Oliver Wyman, a management consulting firm.

Notes: This figure is arranged according to average (avg.) stage length (yellow bar) of a sample of passenger aircraft, arrayed from shortest avg. stage to longest avg. stage length. The blue dots indicate the average cost (in cents) per available seat miles (CASM) flown by aircraft in the sample. The longer the yellow bar, the greater the stage length. Conversely, a high blue dot indicates high a high average CASM, while a low blue dot indicates a lower average CASM.

In addition to the aircraft model, the average number of available seats is shown, as is the type of plane – regional jet (RJ), narrow-body jet (NB), and wide-body jet (WB), The various aircraft models are or were manufactured by the following companies or predecessor companies: CRJ: Bombardier; DC, MD, 7xx: Boeing; ERJ: Embraer; A3xx: Airbus.

In most forecasts, increased demand for new planes is expected to be boosted by the continued growth of low cost carriers (LCCs), by the rapid growth of emerging markets, and by continued market liberalization (access and deregulation). Through 2029, new airplane demand is expected to double, with 56% of deliveries supporting the expansion of air service in growing markets, and 44% of new airplanes replacing older, less efficient airplanes. Boeing projects that replacement of existing aircraft will result in 85% of the fleet having been delivered after 2010.[46]

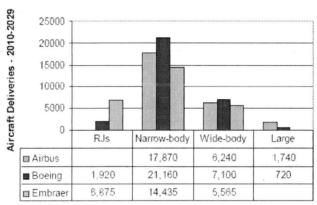

Source: Boeing Commercial Airplanes, Commercial Market Outlook, 2010-2029; Airbus, Global Market Forecast, 2010-2029; Embraer, Market Outlook, 2010-2029.

Notes: The Airbus forecast does not include regional jets. The Embraer forecast combines all twin aisle and large aircraft. Bombardier's forecast includes only the market outlook for turboprop and jet aircraft in the 20- 149 seat range.

Figure 4. Forecast of New Plane Deliveries; 2010-2029.

Boeing, Airbus, and Embraer forecasts vary significantly. Airbus projects a rosier outlook for very large jets (A380s and 747s) than does Boeing: 1,740 deliveries versus 720. At a 2011 list price of US$375.3 million per A380 and about US$201 million per Boeing 747-8/9, the additional sales by Airbus and Boeing for very large aircraft could amount to about $300 billion (at current's prices) if each aircraft maker each sold half of the additional 1,020 large jets forecast by Airbus[47]; Boeing projects that large aircraft sales will amount to $220 million. Airbus, Boeing, Embraer, and Bombardier all project strong demand in the single-aisle, narrow-body category (see Figure 4). According to Boeing 2010–2030 forecast, the number of narrow-body aircraft will more than double, rising from 12,100 to 27,750, or from 62% of the total airplane fleet in 2010 to 70% in 2029 (see Figure 5). Boeing estimates that the market value of narrow-body aircraft sales will amount to $1.95 trillion, or 48% of the $4.0 trillion market for commercial aircraft in 2030.[48]

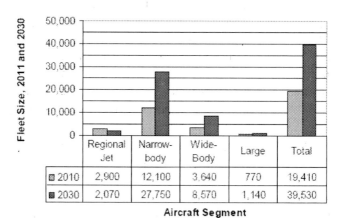

Source: Boeing, Commercial Market Outlook, 2011-2030.

Figure 5. Boeing Forecast – World Fleets by Aircraft Size; 2011 and 2030.

HAS THE BOEING/AIRBUS RIVALRY LEFT THE NARROW-BODY MARKET OPEN TO NEW COMPETITORS?

The single-aisle, narrow-body aircraft segment of the market is directly affected by larger and smaller aircraft programs, which influence investment decisions and competition among aircraft manufacturers. Manufacturers carefully consider their use of capital, labor, and engineering and manufacturing resources, and prioritize their projects accordingly. The ongoing or potential programs of competitors also receive scrutiny. A manufacturer that is developing a new plane will probably not take on additional projects that cannot be handled with available resources unless it believes it must do so to gain a competitive edge or to protect its market.

In the case of the Boeing/Airbus rivalry, there has been a willingness by both companies to pursue strategic goals that have involved attempts to outflank or pre-empt market segments. This has frequently led both companies to take on multiple projects to maintain parity or gain a competitive edge, with the two companies frequently producing similar families of planes. This strategy is not new: Douglas Aircraft, Lockheed, and Boeing earlier fought similar battles in the commercial sphere. One of the consequences of the three-way competition was oversupply of "me too" aircraft, especially large aircraft, and, with the arrival of Airbus, the exit of Lockheed from commercial production and Douglas Aircraft's merger with McDonnell, which effectively eliminated Boeing's U.S. commercial rivals, but left it with a single, stronger European challenger that had strong political and financial support from the governments of France, Germany, the UK, and Spain.[49]

An intense competition between Boeing and Airbus in large wide-body aircraft (A380/747-8 and 787/A350) absorbed significant resources during most of the last decade.[50] But competition in the very large, large, and medium aircraft market segments has been a normal pattern for companies that manufacture advanced commercial aircraft. The drivers of these programs are rising fuel prices, strong demand for more efficient, quieter, and less polluting aircraft, and growing demand for air travel.

Whether the Boeing/Airbus competition in the wide-body market has had any overall effect on their narrow-body aircraft programs is arguable. Some airlines have pressed Boeing to develop a replacement for the 737 that incorporates the technologies that are used on the Boeing 787 (composite materials, newer flight deck technologies, new wing designs, and improved engines, among other features).[51] However, Boeing's experience with production delays, supplier delays, cost overruns, and technical problems in the 787 program has resulted in estimated cost overruns of at least $12 billion more than Boeing's initial target development cost of $5 billion.[52] Whether these technologies can be adapted to smaller planes at a cost that airlines could absorb is a significant part of debate over the futures of both the 737 and A320 programs.

Can Boeing and Airbus Stay Ahead of New Competitors?

The most recent additions to the 737 and A320 families are relatively fuel efficient, operate over longer distances, and carry more passengers than earlier models. Boeing and Airbus will each probably spend more than $10 billion to develop replacement planes, but both appear to be somewhat hesitant to rush into full-scale replacement programs while their current jets remain popular. Airbus, in particular, has raised a concern that the technologies needed for a significantly improved narrow-body aircraft may not be available until the mid-2020s; instead, it has announced that it will re-engine the A319, A320, and A321 by the end of 2015, at an estimated cost of $3 billion.

Boeing had been reluctant to pursue the new engine approach because it would cost several billion dollars without providing Boeing with a new replacement airplane that would deliver the greater efficiencies that customers want.[53] In defending a replacement for the 737 over reengining the current generation 737, James McNerny, Boeing's CEO, said in February 2011, "Putting our backlog at risk twice, once with re-engining, not to mention the cost, and then with the new airplane, only makes sense if it's required in the 2025 timeframe. We are preserving the option if we're wrong - but I don't think so."[54] However, after sales momentum shifted heavily in favor of the re-engined Airbus A320neo during the first half of 2011 (with an order backlog of 1,029 aircraft, including 667 orders announced during the Paris Air Show in June), Boeing came under pressure to provide customers with a re-engined 737 (dubbed the "737RE").

American Airlines (AA), with an all-Boeing fleet, reportedly entered into negotiations with Airbus in March 2011 for the replacement of its fleet of 271 aging MD-80s and 124 Boeing 757s.[55] On July 20, 2011, at a press conference held jointly with Boeing and Airbus, AA announced that it was splitting its order between Airbus and Boeing after Boeing agreed to deliver a re-engined 737, using the CFM International (GE/Safran) LEAP-X engine – one of the two available options for the Airbus 320neo.[56] The 460-aircraft order, the largest ever, is valued at $40 billion. AA will buy or lease 130 A320s, 130 A320neos, 100 737NGs, and 100 737REs, with deliveries of current generation models beginning in 2013. Airbus will begin deliveries of A320neos in 2017 with final deliveries expected in 2022. A decision on Boeing's schedule for delivering its re-engined 737 has not yet been determined.[57]

One major benefit that AA gained was "approximately $13 billion of committed financing provided by the manufacturers through lease transactions that will help maximize balance sheet flexibility and reduce risk. The financing fully covers the first 230 deliveries."[58] Although AA's purchase of A320s could be viewed as a defeat for Boeing, Gerald Arpey, the president and CEO of American, said that such a large number of aircraft could not reasonably have been delivered by a single manufacturer in the timeframe required by American. Splitting the order between Airbus and Boeing provided AA with some earlier delivery slots that will presumably be created by expanding A320 and 737 production capacity. The negotiations with American Airlines also forced Boeing to make a decision in favor of re-engining rather than building a new replacement plane by the end of the decade – a win for Washington state (with its Boeing 737 production lines), and Kansas (where Spirit AeroSystems builds the 737 fuselage).[59] Delta Air Lines, which is also expected to place a large order for narrow-body jets, reportedly also put pressure on Boeing to re-engine its 737 in response to the A320neo.[60] Delta, formerly an all-Boeing airline, began flying Airbus A320s and A330s as a result of its merger with Northwest Airlines in 2008. Like American, Delta could also split its order between Boeing and Airbus. The result for Boeing and Airbus is overflowing order books that may carry 737 and A320 production into the 2020s.

Although the new entrants into narrow-body production believe their products will have distinct advantages over the re-engined Boeing/Airbus products, high demand for the A320neo at the Paris Air Show by numerous international air carriers, the American Airlines order, and the expected large order by Delta Air Lines in the near future, suggest that many air carriers may be taking a wait-and-see approach toward the new competitors.

Is There a Really a Market Opening for New Competitors?

The most significant effect of the two-way Boeing/Airbus competition may be that it has created a perception that the current narrow-body offerings by Boeing and Airbus are outdated. In contrast to this perception, the 737-700/800/900 series and the Airbus A320/A321 models are significantly larger capacity planes that can fly greater distances than earlier models (see Figure 6, which shows the transcontinental reach of the 737NG family). The additional range, greater number of seats, and history of continuous incremental improvements, as well as major upgrades to engines, wings, cockpits, and interiors have allowed Boeing and Airbus to continue to reduce the cost per available seat mile (see Figure 3) on its 737s and A320s. The 737-800, for instance can carry 162 to 189 passengers, while the 737-900ER can carry 180 to 215 passengers. The Airbus A320 can carry 150 to 180 passengers, while the larger A321 can carry 185 to 220 passengers.

There is also perception that the market for 100-149-seat jet aircraft has been all but abandoned by Boeing and Airbus, thus leaving an opening for new entrants. As to the supposed 100-149-seat "gap," there are several issues that cast the entire "gap" debate into question: Is there a need for such a new jet aircraft in emerging markets? If so, Bombardier, Embraer, Boeing, and Airbus all appear to be the companies best positioned to exploit the 100-149 seat gap.

The Chinese appear to be more interested in using its C919 as an entry point to build larger, wide-body civil aircraft.

Whether new, smaller (100-150 seat) narrow-body aircraft can profitably provide the increased fuel efficiency necessary to serve short-haul markets in many of the countries where air travel is expected to grow fastest may depend on jet fuel prices. Additionally, a new generation of larger, quieter (70-90 seat) *turboprop* airplanes, such as the Bombardier Q Series and the ATR 72,[61] can operate more efficiently on short-haul flights than the most efficient small jets – especially where passenger volumes are thin. The larger, more efficient turboprops are equally capable of replacing some smaller jets on short-haul U.S. and European routes.

The 100-150-seat jet aircraft currently being sold or marketed are capable of flying greater distances (2,000 – 6,400 miles) with increased passenger capacity (up to 150 seats). But the larger 737-800/900s and A320/A321 are capable of carrying more than 150 passengers at a lower cost per available seat mile than jets in the 100-150-seat range. Demand for the smaller Boeing and Airbus narrow-body jets has declined as airlines have shifted toward the more efficient Boeing 737-800 and 737-900ER models and Airbus A320s and A321s.

Embraer, traditionally a manufacturer of small regional jet aircraft, move into the lower end of the small narrow-body space in 2005/2006, with the E-190 and E-195. These airplanes seat 94-114 and 108-122 passengers, respectively. Embraer's E-Jet series has sold well and is flown by low-cost carriers, some legacy carriers, and a number of foreign airlines. Bombardier plans to deliver its CSeries jet in 2013, with two variants that will have 100-125 seats and 125-145 seats. Significantly, the Chinese and Russian narrow-body jets will not compete in the 100-150 seat market. Instead, they will compete directly against the largest narrow-body jets in the 737 and A320 series. The Chinese COMAC C919 will have 156-190 seats[62] and the Russian UAC/Irkut MS-21 will have 150-212 seats.[63]

The entry of Chinese, Russian, Canadian, and Brazilian competitors into the narrow-body segment has already forced both Airbus and Boeing to respond to increased competition. The Airbus A320 re-engining program is expected to provide an interim solution that allows it to sell a more fuel-efficient airplane beginning in late 2015 – just before COMAC and UAC/Irkut deliver their first narrow-body jets.[64] However, it appears that the Airbus decision was more directly aimed at Boeing. Its decision to re-engine the A320 was pragmatic because the A320 series (with the exception of the A318) was designed to be re-engined, whereas the 737 can only be reengined by

Challenge to the Boeing-Airbus Duopoly in Civil Aircraft 63

lengthening the landing gear or by using a smaller CFM LEAP-X engine. Because reengining the A320 can be accomplished in five years, Airbus took the lead and airlines, desperate for greater fuel efficiency, responded quickly.

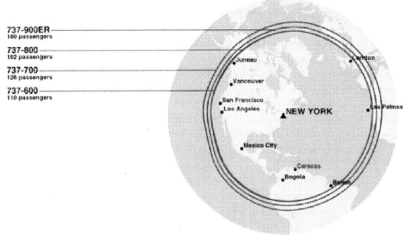

Source: Boeing Commercial Airplanes.
http://www.boeing.com/commercial/737family/pf/pf_rc_newyork.html

Figure 6. Boeing 737 Range Capabilities from New York with Full Passenger Payloads.

While Airbus and Boeing landed billions of dollars in new orders at the Paris Air Show, the Chinese, Russian, Canadian, and Brazilian aircraft manufacturers apparently gained little. Bombardier announced a 30-order deal for the CSeries, but apparently could not conclude a deal with Qatar. Six customers have placed a total of 113 firm orders for the CSeries planes. The Russian-built Sukhoi Superjet gained one order for 12 planes, and China's COMAC reportedly signed an agreement with Ryanair to be a development partner, although it is unclear whether Ryanair will eventually buy the C919. Embraer's chief executive officer, Frederico Curado, said, "Going up against Boeing and Airbus in head-to-head competition is really tough, not only because of their size, but because of their existing product line and industrial capacity. They can have a very quick response and literally flood the market."[65]

While anticipated demand for narrow-body aircraft is high, there is also the larger question of whether the market can accommodate four-to-six firms competing to sell narrow-body aircraft. The decision by Airbus and Boeing to re-engine their A320/737 families appears to have prevented any erosion of sales and has created a cushion against the challengers. With the combined experience that both Boeing and Airbus have in building mainline narrow-body, wide-body, and very large jet aircraft, neither appears ready to take risks that the newcomers have apparently embraced; that is, manufacturing a more efficient aircraft than the 737 or A320. Boeing and Airbus appear to have protected and extended their franchises from an untested group of competitors.

Will China's Market for Aircraft Remain Open to Competition?

The Chinese market is projected to be one of the major drivers for all civil aircraft manufacturers through 2029. Boeing's *Commercial Market Outlook 2010-2029* forecasts that demand for new planes could total 4,330 units worth $480 billion (in 2009 dollars). Single-aisle, narrow-body jets are projected to account for 71% of new deliveries (or 3,090 planes). In contrast, regional jet deliveries are projected to total 280, or 6% of new deliveries – a relatively small number. The Chinese fleet of civil aircraft is expected to increase from 1,570 planes in 2009 to 5,180 planes in 2029, with single-aisle mainline jets increasing from 1,170 to 3,770 between 2009 and 2029 (See Figure 7 for more detail).

The Asia Pacific region is forecast to account for a third of all new plane deliveries during the next 20 years. Although this figure is below total deliveries to slower-growing North America and Europe (which together will account for 13,390 deliveries, or 47% of new plane deliveries), the fleet growth rate for the Asia Pacific region is projected at 5.6% (including China at 6.2%), compared to North America at 1.6% and Europe at 2.3%.[66] So rapidly growing markets are likely to be a major focus for aircraft manufacturers and suppliers, even as slower growth in mature markets continues to produce a significant number of aircraft replacement sales. One major issue for Western aircraft manufacturers and suppliers in the future is their access to the Chinese aircraft market. To date, Western aircraft manufacturers and suppliers have expressed concerns about the protection of their intellectual property and their ability to sell commercial jets in sectors with competing domestic products.

Some Western aircraft manufacturers and suppliers, however, take the view that participation in a Chinese-backed joint venture may boost sales, especially if they expect government-owned airlines to purchase what the central or provincial governments tell them to buy. However, this strategy has not always worked: Embraer, for instance, established a joint venture with

Harbin, a subsidiary of state-owned China Aviation Industry Corporation (AVIC), to manufacture ERJ-145 regional jets in China. The ERJ-145 program produced an average of only 5 planes a year (a disappointingly small number). With the conclusion of the ERJ-145 program in April 2011, Embraer had hoped to manufacture and sell its larger Embraer 190 E-Jet in China. However, the company was blocked by AVIC, which viewed a Chinese-built Brazilian jet as a competitor to the AVIC-designed 90-seat ARJ21 regional jet. Whether the ARJ21 will be accepted by consumers is unknown.

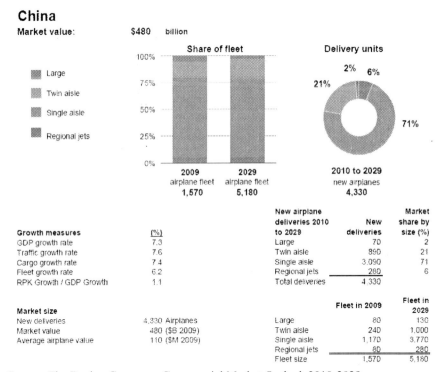

Source: The Boeing Company, Commercial Market Outlook 2010-2029.

Figure 7. China's Market for Civil Aircraft; 2009-2029.

Unlike Embraer's difficulty with regional jets, Bombardier and COMAC have signed an agreement to cooperate on future plane development, marketing, and customer support. The agreement includes sharing of parts between the CSeries and the C919. Additionally, Bombardier has outsourced production of the CSeries fuselage to a subsidiary of AVIC.[67] According to a recent press release announcing the agreement, "This long-term strategic cooperation agreement is based on both COMAC's and Bombardier's desire to build on the potential complementary nature of their products and respective expertise. This includes exploring collaboration in their marketing, customer relationship and customer support strategies to help each other increase overall market share in emerging and mature markets."[68] The resulting planes may share many commonalities, with a view to achieving interoperability among CSeries/C919 aircraft. The 100- 200-seat span of the Bombardier/COMAC planes also offers the potential for a credible challenge to the Boeing/Airbus duopoly and may reduce Boeing and Airbus sales in the China market.[69]

NEW SINGLE-AISLE, NARROW-BODY MARKET ENTRANTS: A BRIEF PROFILE

Bombardier CSeries

The Bombardier CSeries jet is the only mainline plane currently in development that specifically targets the 100-149 seat market.[70] It will come in two versions that cover the alleged gap (or current lack of demand): the CS100 will seat between 100 and 125 passengers and the CS300 will seat between 125 and 145 passengers. Bombardier claims that the CS100 enter into service in 2013 and the CS300 will enter service in 2014. Bombardier's 2011- 2030 forecast for the 100-149 seat commercial jet market calls for 7,000 deliveries over the next 20 years, with the retirement of 3,000 (57%) of the current 100-149-seat fleet. The total fleet of 100-149 seat jets is projected to grow from 5,200 units in 2010 to 9,200 by 2030.[71] Bombardier's competitors in the CS100 (100-125 seats) segment include the Airbus A318 and A319 and Embraer's 190 and 195 aircraft. At a future date, it may also include a stretched Russian-built Sukhoi Superjet 100.

COMAC C919

The COMAC C919 is frequently compared to the Airbus A320, possibly because Airbus has been assembling A320s and A319s in China since 2008, in partnership with AVIC. COMAC, which was spun off from AVIC in 2008, has signed agreements with a number of U.S. and European suppliers of airframe parts, engines, and various systems that will be critical to the success of the program. CFM International will assemble LEAP-X engines for the C919 in China.[72] GE is also participating in a joint venture with AVIC to develop avionics for the C919.[73]

Whether the plane will achieve the efficiencies that COMAC has promised is an open question: reports that designers have had trouble with the plane's weight have apparently caused some of the major Chinese airlines to hold back on orders. The big three Chinese-owned airlines – China Southern, Air China, and China Eastern – apparently limited their exposure to 20 aircraft each. According to a recent study by the RAND Corporation, "the 'big three' each committed only to purchasing five C919s,"[74] with soft options for the other 45 planes. The apparent hesitation of central-government owned airlines to purchase aircraft built by a state-owned company is due, according to RAND, to an unwillingness to "take on more exposure to a program they regard as risky."[75] General Electric's leasing arm, General Electric Commercial Aviation Services (GECAS) has ordered 10 planes, as has the leasing subsidiary of the China Development Bank.[76]

UAC/Irkut MS-21

The three-version (150, 180, and 210 seats) MS-21 aircraft has been described as "Russia's great hope for the revival of its civil aircraft industry."[77] The MS-21, which the company expects to cost $6.3 billion to develop, is scheduled to enter service in 2016. The Russian government is funding 40% of the MS-21's development costs, with the remainder coming through loans, and from Irkut's parent company, the government-owned UAC. According to the MS-21 chief designer and project director, Andrei Matveyev, the aircraft will include 40% composite content (including a composite wing), weigh 15% less, and achieve 25% improved fuel efficiency over current comparable Boeing or Airbus aircraft.[78] Pratt & Whitney will supply engines, which will also power the A320neo (as one of two available engine options for that plane), the Bombardier CSeries, and the Mitsubishi Regional Jet. Irkut also has numerous U.S. partners supplying various systems for the MS-21. To date, 146 firm orders and 39 options have been placed for the MS-21, with 50 orders from Aeroflot, 50 orders from a Malaysian leasing company, and 46 orders from Russian leasing companies.

Embraer

The Embraer 190 E-Jet has 98-114 seats, while the larger Embraer 195 E-Jet has 108- 122 seats. The first delivery of the E-190 was made in 2005 and the E-195 in 2006. Both planes are comparable to small mainline jets and, together with the Embraer 170/175 E-Jets, were designed specifically to fill what Embraer executives believed to be a gap in the 70-120 seat jet market.

The Embraer E-Jets represented a sharp departure from the RJs on which Embraer had built its reputation. Embraer used the E190 and E195 to beat Bombardier to market with a product that upstaged regional jets of comparable size. By the end of 2010, 266 E-190s had been delivered to low-cost carriers, U.S. legacy airlines, and foreign airlines, with a firm order backlog of 157 planes. During the same period, 61 E-195s were delivered, with a firm backlog of 41 planes.[79] Embraer's chief competitor, Bombardier, delivered its first 100-seat CRJ-1000 regional jet (a stretched CRJ-900) in December 2010. As of January 2011, Bombardier had delivered 9 CRJ1000s and had firm orders for another 40.[80] Whether the Bombardier CSeries will lead Embraer to develop a larger plane is uncertain at this point. Nevertheless, some have speculated that Embraer could develop a new plane in response to Bombardier's challenge to Embraer's E-Jet series.

Sukhoi Superjet 100

The first Sukhoi SJ100 was delivered to Armavia, an Armenian airline, on April 19, 2011, and was almost immediately placed in service. The Superjet 100 has a capacity of 86-103 passengers, depending on its seating configuration. After-sales support for the SJ100 will be provided by SuperJet International, a joint venture formed by Sukhoi and the Italian firm Alenia Aeronautica. Alenia owns 51% and Sukhoi 49% of the joint venture. Alenia also has a 25% stake in Sukhoi Civil Aircraft Co., the manufacturer of the SJ1000. The purpose of SJI is to provide the all important in-service support that airlines depend on. SJI provides pilot training, technical training for maintenance staffs, and operates spare parts warehouses for the SJ100 program. According to *Aviation Week and Space Technology*, "Commercial services also will test whether the program can deliver the promised in-service support, of which many customers are skeptical, given the poor reputation of Russia's aerospace industry in this regard."[81]

COMAC ARJ21

A new Chinese regional jet, the ARJ21 (a 90-seat RJ), which is being manufactured by COMAC in partnership with Bombardier, is based on the McDonnell-Douglas MD-90. All of the COMAC ARJ21's major subsystems were sourced to North American and European suppliers.[82] The project has experienced a number of delays and delivery slipped from 2010 to 2011. The ARJ21 was originally an AVIC project, but was transferred to COMAC when the latter assumed responsibility for commercial aircraft development. It is not clear whether regional jets will remain a focus for COMAC, because most forecasts do not anticipate much growth in the Chinese RJ market.

Large Regional Jet

One regional aircraft, the Japanese Mitsubishi Regional Jet (dubbed the "MRJ")(a 70-90 seat plane), appears to be primarily aimed at the Bombardier/Embraer RJ duopoly.

BOEING AND AIRBUS: RESPONSE TO COMPETITION

The decision by Airbus and Boeing to put new high efficiency engines on their planes will provide airlines with upgraded products that have a reputation for dependability. Although Bombardier, COMAC, and Irkut are building narrow-bodies that represent a more radical departure from the 737 and A320, their programs are inherently riskier and have not yet demonstrated that the promised benefits can be delivered. Many airlines may decide to stay with aircraft that they know. It is too soon to know whether the newcomers will succeed. Bombardier and Embraer have established themselves as successful aircraft manufacturers and the Chinese appear to be determined to build a civil aviation industry that competes directly with Boeing and Airbus. Whether the Russians will succeed in building civil aircraft capable of competing in international markets remains to be seen.

For now, the real competition is between Boeing and Airbus. Neither company appears likely to walk away from the segment of the commercial aviation industry that accounts for almost half of revenues. Although the Boeing/Airbus duopoly in small commercial jets is clearly under challenge, it is not obvious that the civil aircraft market is large enough to sustain as many as five additional competitors. Nevertheless, all of the challengers to the Boeing/Airbus duopoly believe that their ability to compete in the narrow-body segment will be critical to the creation of successful domestic aerospace industries. It is clear that the United States, the European Union, Russia, China, Japan, Brazil, and Canada all consider the aerospace to be commercially and militarily strategic.

End Notes

[1] Civil aircraft include all large civil aircraft, fixed wing general aviation aircraft, and helicopters. Large civil aircraft include all aircraft in commercial use (i.e., those operated by airlines and charter operators). U.S. Department of Commerce, International Trade Administration (ITA), *Flight Plan 2011*, March 2011. p. 3.

[2] Department of Commerce, ITA, "2010 U.S. Exports of Aerospace Vehicles and Equipment," http://trade.gov/wcm/groups/internet/@trade/@mas/@man/@aai/documents/web_content/aero_stat_expqtr.pdf

[3] ITA, *Flight Plan 2011*, pp. 3, 5.

[4] Ibid, p. 3. Based on the latest available data (2008).

[5] "Small commercial jet aircraft" is a misnomer, in that it describes airplanes that can seat from 90-220 passengers. Other terms are equally inapt: "narrow-body" and "single-aisle" are frequently used to describe both small- and medium-sized aircraft, including in this report. Medium, large, and very large aircraft are usually twin-aisle airplanes that seat more than 200 passengers. One medium-sized exception is the now out-of-production Boeing 757, a narrow-body, single-aisle aircraft that seats between 186 and 279 passengers. On the other hand, regional jets are also narrow-body, single-aisle airplanes.

[6] The Boeing Company. *2010 Annual Report*. p. 5.

[7] *Financial Times*, "Boeing and Airbus call time on duopoly," June 21, 2011. In economic theory, a duopoly involves two sellers of either identical or "different but rival goods – goods the demand for which does not depend only on their own price but to a non-negligible extent also on the price of the other good." H. Neisser, "Oligopoly as a Non-Zero-Sum Game," *The Review of Economic Studies*, Vol. 25, No. 1, Oct. 1957. p. 7. Even with an effective prohibition against collusive practices, the entry of additional firms into a market characterized by duopolistic competition could be difficult under conditions where a duopoly has achieved an equilibrium position with respect to maximizing their output and revenues. One implication for new entrants is that they generally will have to provide a superior product at a price that is less than the price charged by the incumbents. However, the incumbents could be expected to respond to increased competition by reducing prices in order to maintain output. This will be true as long as marginal revenues exceed marginal costs. See H. Gregg Lewis, "Some Observations on Duopoly Theory," *The American Economic Review*, Vol. 38, No. 2 (May 1948).

[8] Ibid.

[9] Ibid.

[10] Net orders include total orders minus cancellations.

[11] Boeing, *Annual Report 2010*; Airbus, *2010 Commercial Review*.

[12] Embraer, which delivered 58 E-190s and 17 E-195s in 2010, is competing against Airbus' smallest jet, the A318, which has not experienced strong sales.

[13] With some "regional jets" seating more than 120 passengers, the term "regional jet" has becoming increasingly meaningless. Larger Bombardier and Embraer RJs are classified by Boeing in the same single-aisle category as the Boeing 737 and the Airbus A320 (90 – 175 seats). Thus Boeing definition of RJs accounts for jet airplanes that carry fewer than 90 passengers. According to a 2001 study by the U.S. General Accounting Office (GAO)(since renamed the U.S. Government Accountability Office): "There is no uniformly accepted definition of a regional jet either in the industry or in federal laws and regulations. For example, the Wendell H. Ford Aviation Investment and Reform Act for the 21st Century, P.L. 106-181, variously defines a regional jet as having a maximum seating capacity of "not less than 30 nor more than 75" (sec. 210) or "less than 71" (sec. 231). Within the industry, "regional jet" is sometimes used to describe larger aircraft, such as the Fokker F-100 (107 seats) and Boeing 717 (106 seats), and older-technology aircraft, such as the Fokker F-28 (69 seats) and BAe 146-100 (70-82 seats)." GAO, *Aviation Competition: Regional Jet Service Yet to Reach Many Small Communities*, GAO-01-344, February 2001.

[14] Unless otherwise indicated, this report focuses on single-aisle, narrow-body planes that are similar to all variants of the Boeing 737 and Airbus A320 aircraft. The 737 and A320 are mainline aircraft that are flown on what are considered to be short-to-medium-haul routes by large airlines, such as American or United, or by low cost carriers (LCCs), such as Southwest Airways and JetBlue Airways. Smaller regional jets (RJs), primarily produced by Bombardier of Canada, and Embraer of Brazil, typically carry 35 to 90 passengers and are usually operated by regional and feeder airlines.

[15] Bombardier, "COMAC and Bombardier Sign Strategic Agreement on Commercial Aircraft," Press Release, March 24, 2011; *Bloomberg News*, "Bombardier, China's Comac to Cooperate on Plane Development," March 24, 2011.

[16] *Air Transport Intelligence News*, "Proposed stretch dubbed E-195X by Embraer," January 26, 2010; *Air Transport Intelligence News*, "Embraer kills 195X over range concerns," May 13, 2010.

[17] Telephone conversation with Mauro Kern, Embraer's Executive Vice-President for New Programs, Airline Market, February 14, 2011; *ATW Online*, "Embraer eager for Boeing to make 737 re-engine/replacement decision," May 18, 2011.

[18] Boeing, *Current Market Outlook 2011-2030*.

[19] United States International Trade Commission, *The Changing Structure of the Global Large Civil Aircraft Industry and Market: Implications for the Competitiveness of the U.S. Industry*, Investigation No. 332-384, Publication 3143, November 1998. Footnote 15, p. 2-1.

[20] The parent company of AirTran, AirTran Holdings, Inc., was acquired by Southwest on May 2, 2011 for $1.4 billion. AirTran's fleet comprises 88 Boeing 717s and 52 Boeing 737s. Southwest and AirTran will continue to operate as separate carriers until the Federal Aviation Administration (FAA) grants the airline a Single Operating Certificate, which it is expected to do in February 2012. In addition to the Airtran fleet and network of 69 cities, the asset that Southwest may have prized most was the 31 gates at Hartsfield-Jackson Atlanta International Airport that Airtran controls. With its purchase of AirTran, Southwest has established a presence at the busiest passenger airport in the world.

[21] This is especially true when delivery delays and serious cost overruns occur.

[22] Embraer's 190/195 E-Jet, with 108-122 seats, has sold well, but that plane (a stretched version of the 170/175 E-Jet) cannot be stretched further without degrading its efficiency. Embraer will have to develop a new plane rather than a larger variant if it wants to compete in the 125-200 seat segment of the narrow-body market.

[23] Department of Commerce, International Trade Administration, *Russia: Consolidation of the Aerospace Industry*, 2008. p. 1.

[24] Department of Commerce, International Trade Administration, *Russia: Consolidation of the Aerospace Industry*, 2008. p. 1; Vasigh, Bijan, Ken Fleming, and Liam Mackay. *Foundations of Airline Finance*. Burlington, VT: Ashgate Publishing, 2010. pp. 13-14.

[25] United Aircraft Corporation (UAC) website: http://www.uacrussia.ru/en/investors/shares/.

[26] Department of Commerce, International Trade Administration, *Russia: Consolidation of the Aerospace Industry*, 2008. pp. 1, 3.

[27] Boeing, *Commercial Market Outlook 2010*.

[28] Commercial Aircraft Corporation of China (COMAC) website: http://english.comac.cc/products/ca/pi/index.shtml

[29] Large civil aircraft (LCA) typically refers to aircraft with more than 90 seats. Regional jets (RJs) refer to jets with up to 90 seats, although Embraer and Bombardier both produce aircraft that seat more than 100 passengers.

[30] Boeing Commercial Airplanes, the division that manufactures commercial aircraft, is a subsidiary of The Boeing Company, of Chicago. Airbus SAS is a subsidiary of the European Aeronautic Defence and Space Company EADS, NV (EADS), headquartered in Paris, France.

[31] McDonnell Douglas, which merged with Boeing in 1997, produced a family of narrow-body, single aisle aircraft, beginning with the DC-9 (built between 1965 and 1982; capacity: 90-135), the MD-80 (1980-1999; capacity: 130 and 155 passenger versions), the MD-90 (1995-2000; 153 to 172 seats), and the MD-95/Boeing 717 (1999-2006; 106-117 seats). After the merger, Boeing quickly phased out the MD commercial line, with exception of the MD95, a regional jet that was renamed the 717. Of 2,443 DC-9/MD-80/MD-90/717s placed in service, 1,066 remain in service as passenger or cargo aircraft. Parenthetically, early versions of the Boeing 707, once one of the largest passenger aircraft capable of international travel, carried only 149 passengers. Boeing; Airlinerlist.com (December 2010). Lockheed, another major commercial aircraft manufacturer, exited the commercial aircraft market after its wide-body L-1011 failed to win enough orders.

[32] JetBlue and US Airways operate the Embraer 190 E-Jet. Although the Boeing 737-600 is part of the 737 NextGen series, the last order and delivery for that model was in 2005 and 2006, respectively.

[33] Some 737-200s remain in service, although high fuel prices and maintenance costs are causing airlines to retire the plane. No U.S. airline has flown the plane in the continental United States since 2006, when Delta retired the last of the 40-year old jets. Another jet, the 737-300, is the most popular of the 737 Classic series (737-300/400/500 models) with 1,113 deliveries between 1984 and 1999. Recent discoveries of metal fatigue on some of the 737-300s suggest that the life-span of these planes may be shorter than the manufacturer or airlines anticipated. Southwest has stated its intention to retire its 171 737-300s as it receives 737-800s from Boeing.

[34] Southwest Airlines. *Annual Report, Form 10-K*, February 8, 2011, p. 42. Available seat miles (ASMs) are the number of seats available multiplied by the number of miles flown.

[35] Department of Energy, U.S. Energy Information Administration, *This Week in Petroleum*, "The outlook for transportation fuel markets this summer," April 13, 2011.

[36] Load factors, which measure the number of seats sold in terms of total seats available, is calculated by dividing revenue passenger miles by available seat miles.

[37] Ancillary fees have been a significant source of revenue for airlines. Air fares are subject to a 7.5% excise tax that funds the Airport and Airway Trust Fund. Ancillary fees that airlines

charge for a range of optional services, such as checked and carry-on bags; meals; blankets; early boarding; and seat selection are not subject to the 7.5% excise tax. According to GAO, DOT-reported airline ancillary revenues amounted to $7.8 billion in 2009 – an amount the GAO reports is understated, as well as unreported by airlines to the FAA.GAO also noted that, with the exception of checked baggage fees, many of the charges are not provided to the passenger at the time of ticketing, making it difficult for customers to make price comparisons. U.S. GAO, *Commercial Aviation: Consumers Could Benefit from Better Information about Airline-Imposed Fees and Refundability of Government-Imposed Taxes and Fees*, GAO-10-785, July 2010.

[38] *Aviation Daily*, "Intelligence," April 12, 2011, p. 1. The article's source is TeamSAI, an aviation consulting firm that publishes an annual MRO forecast.

[39] The 737 is a mid-1960s-vintage plane; in 1993, it underwent a major upgrade (new cockpit; redesigned wings, and an improved engine that is 5% more fuel efficient and offers 15% lower maintenance costs). The A320 family (the A318/ 319/320/321) is relatively newer: the A320 entered service in 1987, the A321 in 1994, the A319 in 1996, and the A318 in 2003.

[40] U.S. Department of Transportation, Federal Aviation Administration. *FAA Aerospace Forecast, Fiscal Years 2011- 2031*. p. 24

[41] The Massachusetts Institute of Technology (MIT) Airline Data Project defines *stage length* as "The average distance flown, measure in statute miles, per aircraft departure. The measure is calculated by dividing total aircraft miles flown by the number of total aircraft departures performed" using data collected from airlines by the FAA. *Cost per available seat mile* is a "measure of unit cost in the airline industry. CASM is calculated by taking all of an airline's operating expenses and dividing it by the total number of available seat miles produced." http://web.mit.edu/airlinedata/www/Res_Glossary.html

[42] The A300, a wide-body with a relatively short stage length, had the highest CASM among all the wide-bodies surveyed.

[43] Boeing experienced a lengthy 52-day strike in September and October 2008, when 27,000 workers walked out at facilities in Washington State, Oregon, and Kansas. Aircraft production was halted during the strike. *New York Times*, "Boeing and Union Reach Tentative Deal," October 27, 2008.

[44] Boeing, "Refurbished Boeing 737 Paint Hangar Opens to Meet Rate Increase," Press Release, July 13, 2011.

[45] Data are from the Boeing and Airbus websites. See also *Aviation Daily*, "Boeing Sets 737NG Production Rate At 42/Month," June 16, 2011.

[46] Boeing Commercial Planes, *Current Market Outlook, 2010-2029*.

[47] Prices are from the Airbus and Boeing websites.

[48] Boeing, *Current Market Outlook 2011*. Presentation by Randy Tinseth, Vice President, Marketing, Boeing Commercial Airplanes, Paris, France, June 2011.

[49] This report does not discuss aircraft subsidies (alleged or otherwise) that might have been provided to either Airbus or Boeing. Airbus was organized in 1970 through the actions of the French, German, and British governments; Spain joined in 1971. The company essentially pooled the assets of several aviation companies, all of which were individually too small to compete against Boeing, Lockheed, or McDonnell Douglas.

[50] It has been argued that the Airbus decision to build the very large A380 was designed to kill the smaller 747, a successful plane that has played a significant role in both the long-haul passenger and cargo sectors since 1970. Boeing's response, however, to enlarge and update the 747 with a plane that is larger than the 747-400 but still smaller than the A380 may have

been the appropriate response to Airbus. Some observers believe that the Airbus A380 is a niche product that is too large to operate on any but the longest routes. Proponents of the A380 claim that it is the perfect vehicle for long-haul flights between major hubs. They point to strategies being pursued by Emirates Airline and Singapore Airlines, which use the planes to move passengers through large hubs in Dubai and Singapore that serve as gateways to other destinations using smaller aircraft. Emirates currently has a fleet of 15 Airbus A380s and 53 Boeing 777s for long-haul flights.

[51] *The Seattle Times*, "Southwest wants new fuel-saving 737 version," September 13, 2005. Southwest's acquisition of Airtran Airways, with its mixed fleet of Boeing 717s and 737s, could cause Southwest to rethink its long-time one-fleet strategy. Southwest's vice-president operations coordination center, has said that Boeing's timing on the 737 replacement by 2020 is too late for Southwest, which is looking for a plane that can deliver 25% better efficiency: "We've squeezed the turnip, there's nothing left in the [737]NG. It now goes back to the airframe and the engine. We'll look at re-engining, but we're waiting for someone to tell us what [Boeing is] going to do." *Flight International*, "2020 too late for Southwest 737 replacement," May 12, 2011.

[52] *The Seattle Times*, "Dreamliner's woes pile up," December 18, 2010.

[53] *Aviation Week*. "Single-Aisle Aircraft: Financing Gains Influence," March 21, 2011.

[54] *Aviation Daily*, "Boeing Leans Further Toward 737 Replacement," February 11, 2011.

[55] *ATWOnline (Air Traffic World)*, "Facing pressure from fast-selling A320neo, Boeing's hand forced on 737 re-engining," July 20, 2011.

[56] *SeattlePi.com*, "American Airlines buys Airbus, stings Boeing: Boeing proposes re-engining 737 to get share of 460- jet order," July 20, 2011. According to AMR, the parent of American Airlines, American "will have 365 options and purchase rights for additional [Airbus] aircraft. American has the flexibility to convert its delivery positions into variants within the A320 Family, including the A319 and A321."

[57] One issue posed by the Boeing 737 is its ground clearance. Hanging a larger CFM LEAP-X engine will require that the plane's landing gear be lengthened or that the plane use an engine with a smaller diameter fan blade, which could potentially limit some of the expected efficiency gains. AMR Corporation, AA's parent, stated in its July 20, 2011 Form 8-K Security and Exchange Commission (SEC) filing that it "intends to order 100" Boeing 737REs. American also announced that it is Boeing's launch partner for the re-engined plane.

[58] AMR Corporation. Form 8-K filing, July 20, 2011.

[59] *SeattlePi.com*, "American Airlines buys Airbus, stings Boeing: Boeing proposes re-engining 737 to get share of 460- jet order" July 20, 2011; *The Wichita Eagle*, "Spirit to gain from Boeing's 737 choice," July 21, 2011.

[60] *ATWOnline*, "Facing pressure from fast-selling A320neo, Boeing's hand forced on 737 re-engining," July 20, 2011.

[61] The ATR 72 is manufactured by Avions de Transport Régional (ATR), a joint venture between Alenia (Italy) and EADS.

[62] COMAC website: http://english.comac.cc/products/ca/pi/index.shtml; *MarketWatch*, "Safran, GE win contract for engines to upcoming Chinese jet," December 21, 2009; *Flightgolbal*, "Comac plans six C919 models targeting Airbus and Boeing," November 16, 2010.

[63] Irkut website: http://www.irkut.com/en/services/projects/

[64] *Wall Street Journal*, "Airbus Ends Air Show With Huge Order," June 23, 2011.

[65] Ibid.

[66] Boeing, *Commercial Market Outlook 2010-2029.*

[67] Bombardier, "Bombardier CSeries Aircraft Program Reaches Another Milestone," Press Release, March 25, 2010; *Aviation Daily*. "Aircraft Builders Hit Bumps In China," March 15, 2011.
[68] Bombardier, "COMAC and Bombardier Sign Strategic Agreement on Commercial Aircraft," Press Release, Shanghai. March 24, 2011.
[69] *Aviation Daily*, "Comac, Bombardier Aim For Long-Term Cooperation In Commercial Aircraft," March 28, 2011.
[70] As noted above, the Embraer 190 and 195 E-Jets, which seat 90-122 passengers, have been in service for at least five years.
[71] *Bombardier Commercial Aircraft Market Forecast 2011-2030*, May 18, 2011. p. 11.
[72] *Flightglobal*, "CFM to build LEAP-X engine in China after C919 deal," December 21, 2009.
[73] *Seattlepi.com*, "GE to develop avionics Chinese firm," January 19, 2011.
[74] RAND, Ready for Takeoff: China's Advancing Aerospace Industry, Santa Monica CA: RAND Corporation, 2011. p. 27.
[75] Ibid.
[76] *Aviation Week*, "Hainan, Gecas To Be Early C919 Customers," November 15, 2010.
[77] *Aviation Week and Space Technology*, "Russian Revival," October 18, 2010.
[78] *Air Transport World*, "Irkut calls for MS-21 tenders following design freeze," January 7, 2009.
[79] Embraer, Investor Relations, Highlights, Orderbook. http://www.embraer.com.br
[80] Bombardier, Backgrounder. Program Status Report – Bombardier CRJ Series, January 31, 2011.
[81] *Aviation Week and Space Technology*, "Just How Super?," April 25, 2011. p. 41.
[82] RAND, *Ready for Takeoff: China's Advancing Aerospace Industry*, Santa Monica CA: RAND Corporation, 2011. p. 26.

INDEX

#

21st century, 3, 6
9/11, 53

A

access, 17, 20, 24, 28, 45, 57, 64
accounting, 23
acquisitions, 15, 16, 19
adjustment, 20, 21
aerospace, vii, 37, 38, 39, 40, 41, 42, 43, 45, 52, 53, 68, 70
aerospace industry, vii, 37, 39, 41, 53, 68
Africa, 15, 33
air carriers, 61
aircraft parts, vii, 37, 39
airline industry, 53, 73
airline mergers, 46
amortization, 53
annual rate, 49
antidumping, 24
Asia, 42, 64
assets, 15, 28, 33, 54, 73
authorities, 13, 17, 51
aviation industry, 55, 69

B

baggage, 53, 73
balance sheet, 60
banking sector, 3
banks, 7, 32, 34
bargaining, 10
base, 28, 31
batteries, 16
bauxite, 26
Beijing, 32, 34
benefits, 36, 51, 53, 69
blueprint, 18
bonds, 30
Brazil, 5, 8, 12, 16, 34, 38, 40, 42, 43, 70, 71
bribes, 13
business model, 46
buyer, 12, 14, 15
buyers, 15

C

cabinet, vii, 37, 39
cables, 16
capital markets, 45
carbon, 25, 26
cash, 30

category a, 71
certification, 30
challenges, 27
chemicals, 21, 26, 34
Chicago, 72
China, vii, 1, 2, 3, 4, 5, 6, 7, 8, 9, 10, 11, 12, 13, 14, 15, 16, 17, 18, 19, 20, 21, 22, 23, 24, 25, 26, 27, 28, 29, 30, 31, 32, 33, 34, 35, 36, 38, 40, 42, 43, 44, 49, 50, 51, 63, 64, 65, 66, 67, 70, 71, 72, 75
Chinese firms, 15, 33
Chinese government, 2, 3, 4, 7, 9, 10, 12, 13, 14, 16, 17, 18, 19, 24, 27, 31
Chinese industrial policy, vii, 1
cities, 19, 53, 71
civil aircraft, vii, 37, 38, 39, 40, 42, 44, 46, 49, 52, 62, 64, 67, 69, 70, 72
classes, 41
classification, 43
clean energy, 17, 30, 31
closure, 18, 20
coal, 11, 12
coke, 11, 26
collaboration, 66
commerce, 36
commercial, 13, 38, 39, 40, 41, 42, 43, 44, 45, 47, 49, 50, 51, 52, 53, 55, 58, 59, 63, 64, 66, 69, 70, 72
commodity, 12, 13, 21, 34
Commonwealth of Independent States, 49
Communist Party, 10
communities, 46
community, 14
competition, 2, 38, 41, 44, 46, 48, 58, 59, 61, 63, 69, 70
competitive advantage, 26, 27
competitive markets, 48
competitiveness, 45, 50
competitors, 10, 16, 31, 39, 40, 41, 44, 45, 47, 51, 58, 61, 62, 64, 66, 69
complement, 55
complexity, 46, 47
composition, 10, 18
conference, 60
configuration, 43, 54, 68

Congress, vii, 1, 2, 3, 17, 21, 33, 37, 39
consolidation, 11, 16, 20, 21, 22, 40, 53
construction, 8
consulting, 10, 56, 73
consumers, 65
consumption, 5, 8, 9
cooling, 18
cooperation, 51
coordination, 74
corruption, 13
cost, 2, 12, 14, 16, 31, 46, 47, 53, 54, 56, 59, 60, 61, 62, 67, 68, 71
credit market, 15
crude oil, 12, 53
crude steel, vii, 1, 4, 5, 6, 7, 8, 10, 11, 32
currency, 2, 3, 21, 22, 29, 30, 34, 36
customer relations, 66
customers, 44, 45, 46, 47, 48, 60, 63, 68, 73
CVD, 30

D

Delta Air Lines, 55, 61, 72
Department of Commerce, 36, 70, 72
Department of Energy, 72
Department of Transportation (DOT), 73
deposits, 12, 15, 30
depreciation, 53
depth, 38
deregulation, 46, 57
designers, 67
detention, 13
developed countries, 3, 7
developing countries, 14, 29
direct investment, 2, 28
directors, 28
distribution, 10
domestic demand, vii, 1, 3, 4, 8, 17, 18, 21, 22, 31
domestic economy, 18
domestic resources, 16
dominance, 15, 40
drawing, 42
dumping, 2, 10, 22, 25, 26, 29, 30, 35
duopoly, 38, 40, 66, 69, 70

Index

E

earnings, 51
economic development, 3
economic downturn, 3, 18, 27, 46
economic growth, 3, 6, 7, 9, 22, 23
economic growth rate, 3
economic independence, 50
economic power, 3
economic recession, vii, 1, 3, 6, 7
economic reform, 3, 4
economic relations, 36
economic theory, 70
economics, 54
electric arc furnaces, 33
electricity, 20
emerging markets, 57, 61
employees, 13
employment, viii, 37
encouragement, 15, 16
energy, 2, 11, 15, 27, 31
energy consumption, 2, 27
enforcement, 2, 29, 30, 31
engineering, 51, 58
environment, 10, 15, 27
environmental protection, 24
environmental regulations, 51
equilibrium, 70
equipment, viii, 12, 30, 31, 34, 37, 38, 39, 48, 49, 52
equity, 36
erosion, 64
espionage, 13, 33
ethnicity, 13
Europe, 35, 48, 64
European Union, 20, 22, 23, 26, 35, 70
evidence, 25, 40
excess supply, 9
exchange rate, 3
expertise, 66
export control, 26
export market, 5, 31
export ratio, 22
export subsidies, 20
exporter, 9, 11, 22, 32
exporters, 3, 29, 31
exports, viii, 2, 3, 16, 20, 21, 22, 23, 24, 26, 30, 31, 34, 35, 37, 39
exposure, 67

F

FAA, 55, 71, 73
families, 40, 41, 42, 43, 51, 58, 59, 64
fear, 9, 28, 36, 50
federal law, 71
Federal Register, 26
fertilizers, 21
fiber, 16
financial, 15, 20, 24, 27, 46, 48, 59
financial institutions, 24
financial resources, 20
financial support, 59
flexibility, 46, 60, 74
flight, 41, 59
flights, 46, 53, 55, 62, 74
fluid, 41
force, 12, 30
forecasting, 3
foreign companies, 16, 30
foreign investment, 4
France, 8, 38, 39, 51, 59, 72, 73
franchise, 44
free trade, 50
fuel efficiency, 42, 62, 63, 67
fuel prices, 53, 54, 59, 62, 72
funding, 67
funds, 72

G

GDP, 3, 7
Germany, 5, 8, 23, 32, 59
global competition, 19, 40
global demand, 2
global economy, 12
global recession, 15
goods and services, 30
governments, 20, 31, 41, 50, 59, 64, 73

grants, 24, 31, 71
graph, 56
gratings, 35
grounding, 53
growth, 2, 3, 5, 7, 9, 12, 14, 17, 19, 27, 29, 31, 32, 47, 55, 57, 64, 69
growth rate, 3, 7, 64
Guangdong, 34
Guangzhou, 34
guidance, 19, 55
guidelines, 10
Guinea, 14
Gulf Coast, 54

H

health, 2, 18, 22
height, 41
history, 41, 61
Hong Kong, 15
host, 27, 45
hub, 46
hybrid, 16

I

imported products, 4
imports, 2, 4, 11, 12, 14, 16, 19, 22, 23, 24, 25, 29, 33, 50
improvements, 47, 61
impurities, 11, 12
increased competition, 62, 70
incumbents, 39, 70
independence, 50
India, 5, 8, 12, 22, 32, 42
indirect effect, 47
industrial policies, 26, 50
industrial policy, vii, 1
industrialization, 8, 11, 31
industrialized countries, 4, 6, 27
industries, 2, 4, 18, 26, 30, 34, 44, 70
industry, vii, 1, 2, 4, 6, 10, 11, 12, 13, 16, 17, 18, 19, 20, 23, 24, 25, 27, 28, 31, 32, 34, 37, 39, 41, 49, 50, 53, 55, 67, 68, 71

industry consolidation, 19, 20
inflation, 3
infrastructure, 3, 8, 28, 55
initiation, 26
intellectual property, 50, 51, 64
intellectual property rights, 50, 51
international trade, 2, 22
International Trade Administration, viii, 38, 39, 70, 72
interoperability, 66
investment, 12, 13, 15, 19, 20, 27, 28, 29, 36, 55, 58
investment capital, 27
investments, 15, 45
investors, 15, 34, 72
Iran, 8
Ireland, 47
iron, 2, 10, 11, 12, 13, 14, 15, 16, 18, 19, 20, 27, 31, 33
issues, vii, 2, 3, 17, 22, 31, 34, 35, 36, 61
Italy, 5, 8, 74

J

Japan, 5, 6, 8, 22, 23, 32, 38, 40, 43, 44, 70
joint ventures, 48

K

kill, 73

L

Latin America, 42
law enforcement, 2
laws, 2, 4, 22, 29, 30, 31
legislation, 29
lending, 3
liberalization, 57
light, 34
limestone, 11
loans, 7, 16, 24, 31, 34, 67
local government, 3, 10
logistics, 34

Index

longevity, 52
low cost carriers, 57, 71
lower prices, 14
Luxemburg, 5

M

magnesium, 26
magnitude, 6, 22
majority, vii, 1, 22, 27
man, 70
management, 10, 12, 51, 56
manganese, 26
manipulation, 29, 30
manufacturing, vii, 2, 11, 16, 27, 28, 31, 34, 36, 37, 38, 39, 40, 41, 42, 43, 49, 50, 58, 64
marginal costs, 70
marginal revenue, 70
market access, 50
market economy, 30
market segment, 41, 48, 58, 59
market share, 44, 48, 50, 66
marketing, 50, 65
materials, 2, 26, 31, 53, 59
media, 13, 36
melting, 11
mergers, 15, 19
metals, 3, 16, 21, 30, 34
methodology, 30
Mexico, 8, 23, 26, 35
migration, 28
military, 16, 38
models, 41, 44, 47, 51, 55, 56, 59, 60, 61, 62, 72, 74
modernization, 55
momentum, 60

N

NAFTA, 23
national policy, 50
national security, 17, 28, 36
natural resources, 14, 17, 27, 31

negative effects, 46
negotiating, 10
net exports, viii, 37, 39
NextGen, 72
North America, 33, 48, 64, 69
Northwest Airlines, 61

O

Obama Administration, 29, 30, 36
officials, 2, 22, 28, 29
oil, 28, 34, 53
openness, 38
operating costs, 53, 54
operations, 16, 46, 74
opportunities, 19, 29, 50
ores, 12, 13, 33
overlap, 41
overproduction, 21
overseas investment, 29
ownership, 51
oxygen, 10

P

Pacific, 64
parity, 58
participants, 39
passenger airline, 48
petroleum, 72
phosphorus, 26
plants, 16
playing, 34
Poland, 8
policy, 16, 17, 19, 20, 34, 36
policy makers, 17, 38, 39, 55
political power, 3
pollution, 19
power plants, 11
PRC, 34
president, 25, 40, 60, 74
President, vii, 28, 36, 37, 39, 71
President Obama, vii, 37, 39
principles, 50

probe, 33, 35, 36
producers, 2, 4, 6, 10, 14, 15, 21, 22, 24, 25, 26, 27, 31, 33, 35, 41, 43, 44
product life cycle, 47
production costs, 18, 19, 31
production quota, 16
profit, 45
profitability, 9, 12, 17, 31
project, 14, 32, 36, 57, 67, 69
promote innovation, 51
protection, 64

Q

questioning, 13
quotas, 2, 16, 17, 22, 24, 26

R

rare earth elements, 16, 31, 34
raw materials, 2, 4, 11, 15, 16, 17, 20, 26, 31, 35
reality, 6
recession, vii, 1, 3, 6, 7, 46, 53, 55
reciprocity, 27
recommendations, iv
recovery, vii, 1, 3, 9, 21
recycling, 20
reform, 71
regions of the world, 55
regulations, 2, 22, 71
repair, 14, 53
reputation, 48, 49, 68, 69
requirements, 45, 47
resistance, 27
resources, 4, 11, 15, 16, 19, 33, 34, 38, 43, 51, 52, 58, 59
response, 28, 29, 45, 53, 61, 63, 68, 73
response time, 29
restrictions, 2, 26, 31, 35
restructuring, 16, 21
retaliation, 50
retirement, 42, 66
revenue, 48, 72

rights, 74
risk, 45, 48, 50, 60
risks, 7, 44, 45, 51, 64
routes, 46, 53, 62, 71, 74
rules, 25, 30, 31, 35, 36
Russia, 5, 8, 16, 22, 23, 34, 38, 40, 42, 43, 44, 49, 67, 68, 70, 72

S

safety, 2, 4, 12, 22, 29, 35, 38, 45, 50, 51
sanctions, 36
scale economies, 50
scandium, 34
scope, vii, 26, 37, 39
security, 28
sellers, 70
Senate, 2
service industry, viii, 38, 39
services, 10, 40, 53, 68, 73, 74
shock, 53
silicon, 26
Singapore, 74
snaps, 33
solution, 62
South Africa, 8
South Korea, 5, 8, 12, 14, 22, 23, 32
Soviet Union, 4, 48
Spain, 8, 59, 73
speculation, 3, 13
spending, 38, 53
spot market, 14
spreadsheets, 56
stability, 18, 19
state, 10, 13, 16, 17, 24, 27, 28, 33, 38, 42, 43, 45, 50, 61, 65, 67
state-owned enterprises, 16
states, 16, 29, 35
statistics, vii, 1, 7, 11, 22, 23
statutes, 29
statutory authority, 36
steel, vii, 1, 2, 3, 4, 5, 6, 7, 8, 9, 10, 11, 12, 13, 14, 15, 16, 17, 18, 19, 20, 21, 22, 23, 24, 25, 26, 27, 28, 29, 31, 32, 33, 34, 35, 36

steel industry, vii, 1, 2, 3, 4, 5, 9, 10, 11, 13, 15, 17, 19, 21, 22, 23, 24, 27, 31, 32, 33, 34
stimulus, 3, 7, 17
strategic cooperation, 66
stress, 15
stretching, 44
structure, 10, 12, 17, 18, 19
supplier, 11, 16, 17, 59
suppliers, 14, 15, 23, 38, 41, 44, 45, 50, 51, 64, 66, 69
support services, 48
surging, 11
surplus, viii, 2, 3, 5, 21, 37, 39

T

Taiwan, 8, 12, 22
target, 17, 33, 59
tax cuts, 24
taxes, 16, 17, 24
technological advancement, 20
technologies, 20, 28, 50, 59
technology, 4, 10, 11, 16, 19, 20, 27, 31, 36, 71
tension, 20
time-frame, 45
total product, 12, 23
trade, viii, 2, 3, 4, 10, 12, 13, 18, 20, 22, 24, 25, 26, 28, 29, 30, 31, 34, 35, 36, 37, 39, 70
trade agreement, 36
trade policy, 20, 26
trading partners, 20, 22
training, 46, 68
training programs, 46
transactions, 60
transport, 41, 49
transportation, 72
Treasury, 27, 28, 36
Treasury Secretary, 27
trial, 13, 33
Trust Fund, 72
Turkey, 8

U

U.S. aerospace shipments, vii, 37, 39
U.S. aircraft manufacturing industry, vii, 37, 39
U.S. Department of Commerce, 24, 25, 70
U.S. Geological Survey, 33
Ukraine, 8, 22, 23
unions, 28
unit cost, 73
United Kingdom (UK), 8, 59
United States, v, vii, 1, 2, 3, 5, 6, 8, 16, 20, 21, 22, 23, 25, 26, 27, 30, 31, 35, 36, 37, 38, 39, 48, 70, 71, 72
urbanization, 8, 11, 31

V

value added tax, 10, 24
variables, 55
Venezuela, 15
Vice President, 73
Vietnam, 12
vision, 50
VLA, 41
volatility, 53
vote, 25
vulnerability, 16

W

wages, 53
Washington, 61, 73
weakness, 46
web, 70, 73
websites, 73
White House, 28, 29, 36
wind turbines, 16
workers, viii, 25, 33, 37, 39, 73
workforce, 38
World Trade Organization (WTO), 26, 27, 30, 31, 35, 36
World War I, 4

Y

yttrium, 34

Z

zinc, 26